How Old are We

Shirley Scott

iUniverse, Inc.
Bloomington

How Old are We

iUniverse books may be ordered through booksellers or by contacting:

iUniverse
1663 Liberty Drive
Bloomington, IN 47403
www.iuniverse.com
1-800-Authors (1-800-288-4677)

ISBN: 978-1-4502-7859-1 (sc)
ISBN: 978-1-4502-7860-7 (ebk)

Printed in the United States of America

iUniverse rev. date: 12/13/2010

Preface

In writing this book, I learned a lot about myself, my thought patterns, picking up on other peoples' thoughts and channeling energy but there are still many mysteries in this Universe to discover. Much of what is written here still needs to be studied, investigated and proven. Some of the events I have experience defy everything we know or think we know which makes them a lot of fun, but not very scientific. It's good to have an open mind as you read through the book because there are some things that just can't be proven.

Also, when I refer to the Bible or other text about the Bible it's how I have interrupted what I've read. I perceive the world in a different way than many people and I guess that's what this book is all about.

It's not about being right, wrong or knowing it all. It's about looking at life in a different way and asking yourself questions. It's about what I believe and my everyday life.

My parents raised my sister, brother and I with equal love and respect. They treated us as individuals and never asked us to be like the other or anyone else for that matter. They were very wise parents and open to many unexplained phenomenon. Maybe that's why I'm very open to what I experience, see and hear. I don't judge it. I just run it by my higher self to see if it'll work for me.

I want to thank Skip who read this and helped edit it. He's from a scientific background and has to have most things shown or proven to him. He is one of my best friends and I love him dearly, even if we think differently. After all, this world is about being different and accepting those differences for what they are.

I'm hoping this book will excite you about the world we live in and the worlds we don't live in. I hope it peaks your interest enough that you go exploring on your own about your world and the truth of your world.

I don't pretend to know all the answers to all the questions. Sometimes we just have to go with the fact we "feel" something or "know" something even if it can't be proven. Each of us has our own truths, lies, feelings, opinions and emotions that we have to explore and understand; that's what this book is about. It's about moving away from trusting "blind faith" and walking into intelligent guidance. It's about thinking before you act. It's about knowing different things without understanding where that "knowing" comes from.

The book is about recognizing who we are, where we might have come from, what our soul does and how old it really could be.

So with out further delay, I'll start at the beginning and work toward another beginning because I don't believe there's an end.

Contents

How It All Started

When I asked the Universe to help me bring the knowledge of my soul forward, I never thought it would lead to how I live my life today or the things I do and see.

Some of the things you are going to read will seem crazy. Or they might seem "too far out there" for you to believe or even comprehend. All I can ask is you try to have an open mind, a loving heart and see what resonates with you as you read what was channeled through me to write this book.

As you read what has happened to me, you might even start your own remembering process of what you have experienced in this life time and what your soul holds in its memory banks from past lives. What doesn't resonate with you means you haven't experienced it, you don't remember or you were somewhere else in time and space when it was happening to me.

Remember, I'm writing about my experiences. These are experiences and lessons I've had in my world at a certain time and in a certain place. It's not about being right or wrong or even understanding it all. It's what my soul, spirit guides, angels and teachers on the other side are telling me to write.

Before I get started, you might like to know something about me. I didn't start out as a clairvoyant and animal communicator. I was just another ordinary person from Portland, Oregon. I lived my life pretty much like everyone else I knew. I was married for 25 years to an abusive alcoholic, raised two children and then got a divorce. I believe the divorce was the beginning of a new life for me.

By Feb. 2000, I had survived my painful marriage and rough divorce, cervical cancer and a hysterectomy and thought I wouldn't need to experience too much more in the way of excitement in my life. But the powers above had one more surprise for me.

It was very sudden and I wasn't prepared for it. I had fought cancer and won. I had survived sexual abuse from the age of 4 until I was 9 years old by a step-grandfather. I had survived physical and mental abuse in a dysfunctional marriage but watching your body die from an observers' point of view is something no one is ready for.

I had never been allergic to anything in my life but on February 10, 2000, I was to learn just how quickly an allergy can come on. I had been one of those lucky people who could eat anything at anytime and never have it upset my stomach or system. I really never paid attention to what I ate.

All that changed the day I popped a mint sweeten with Aspartame into my mouth. Within seconds I knew something was wrong. I could feel my face getting hot. I looked in the mirror saw and red welts forming on my cheeks. My tongue had doubled in size and I instinctively knew I was dying. It was a very strange feeling, knowing you are dying and there's really nothing you can do about it.

I dialed 911 knowing the fire house and rescue units were only 3 blocks from my house. Within seconds, I heard the sirens rushing my way. Then they stopped just outside my front door. I stumbled toward the front door. It was hard to stand because my blood vessels were already shutting down in my feet and legs and they felt like they were on fire. I blindly found the door knob, turned it and pulled the door open.

I knew the paramedics were standing there but I couldn't see them. The blood vessels in my eyes were collapsing and all I could see was colored lights. I heard the concern in their voice as they looked at my swollen face. My tongue was now protruding out of my month and I couldn't talk. I turned and fumbled my way back to my living room where I found a chair and sat down. I felt for the tin of mints and I handed it to them. Then I blacked out.

The next thing I remember, I was in a peaceful place. I seemed to be floating in a wonderful white cloud of Light about three feet off the ground and just to the right of my body, which was now lying on the floor. I had no idea how my body had gotten there. The last thing I remembered was sitting in the chair at my dining room table trying to talk to the paramedics. The pain was gone and I could see again. I felt great!

The paramedics were working on my lifeless body as they hooked up wires to my chest and put an oxygen mask over my nose and mouth. Tourniquets were placed on my upper arms. I watched as the paramedics tried to find a vein so they could save my life. They were in a panic but I was very calmly watching the whole situation.

The paramedic on my left was beating my arm below the tourniquets and saying, "I can't find a vein."

"Now that's just plan crazy," I remember thinking. "I have great veins." My next thought was, "Great, my body's dying and they send someone who can't see a vein."

The paramedic on my right was taking my blood pressure under the tourniquet. Now if you know anything about taking your blood pressure, you know that any tension or pressure on your arm will restrict the blood flow and you'll get an untrue reading. I knew the tourniquet on my arm should make my blood pressure register very high.

I had no more gotten this thought out of my head, or however I was "thinking" in this white cloud of air, then the paramedic said, "Her pressure is 69 over 38 and falling fast."

"Wow", I thought. "I'm really dying. So this is what it's like to die." I felt no panic, pain or anxiousness. I just felt peace, love and comfort but that changed when I saw a third paramedic get out the chest paddles.

"How long to code?" He asked the paramedic on my right.

"30 seconds at this rate." Was the answer.

"Holy smoke!" was all I could think. "I don't want these guys using those paddles on my chest – they'll leave marks!" I didn't seem to care that I was dying but to have marks on my body, that bothered me!

This was the first time I had thought about going back into my body. Up until this point, it had been very interesting from my spectators' point of view. But the paddles were a different stories. With one giant thought I said, "I don't want them to use that on me."

That's when I heard a voice behind me say, "Then go back and stay conscious."

I thought back to the voice, "I can do that." And before I could turn to see who I was talking too, I was headed back to my body.

I slammed back into my body so hard I remember yelling, which scared the paramedic on my left because I felt him jump.

He yelled, "I've got a vein!" and I felt the jab of a needle going into my hand. Suddenly I felt a cool liquid running into my veins. The paramedics were literally pushing saline solution through a tube and into my veins to get them open. Within a few minutes I was on a stretcher and heading out the door to the wanting ambulance. I almost felt like Cinderella except for all the tubes coming out of my body. Needless to say, I'm alive to tell the story today. The near-death, out-of-body experience was great but it was what happened next that really turned my life into what it is today.

It only took a good nights rest in the hospital and I was back to my old self the next day. At least that's what I thought, until I got home. I walked into my front room and felt like something was different or someone was there hiding. Then out of nowhere an outline of a person appeared on the front room wall. I watched as it developed into a full shadowy figure of a woman. I got the feeling it was some kind of a spirit coming through the wall and floating into my front room.

Then I heard a voice in my head that said, "Don't be afraid. I'm here to show you what you're going to be able to see from now on."

I didn't feel afraid but I thought I might be going nuts. I thought there must be something wrong with me or all the medications they had given me in the hospital hadn't left my system. I just stood there and stared at this wonderful Light being that was standing in front of me. Then I blinked and I found I was again staring at a blank wall. The shadowy figure had vanished.

The next day I told myself that I had a great imagination and whatever I thought I'd seen was certainly a figment of that imagination.

A few months before this I had been in Mexico on my first spiritual retreat and had seen my first aura (an aura is the energy light or life force around our head and body) but I hadn't seen any spirits walk through walls. So I told myself this wasn't really happening. I ignored it and went on my merry way. I knew I had experienced something but I wasn't about to tell anyone about it. Besides at this stage of my learning I was unsure who I could tell and not have them think I was crazy.

It wasn't more than a couple of days later when I realized I knew some things were going to happen before they happened. One day I over-heard someone talking about having an upset stomach. I received a very clear picture of a pepperoni pizza and knew they pepperoni had been bad.

When I told the lady what I was feeling, she said, "How did you know I had pizza?" That's when I knew I had to find out what was happening to me. I also knew I had to very careful about what I said to people.

I started looking for help. I didn't know who to talk to or who I could tell without them thinking I was nuts. So I called a friend of mine who believed in these things and told her what was going on. She just laughed and thought it was the most wonderful thing she had ever heard. (Of course she would because it wasn't happening to her.)

"Why don't you see if there's a school near you that helps new psychics understand what's happening to them?" She asked.

"I'm not psychic!" I answered almost in a panic. I was a business woman in a company that wouldn't take kindly to their top sales manager being psychic. I was still in the belief system that "told" me my job was my life.

"Well, you can fight it or you can do what the Universe has planned for you. The choice is yours." she said.

The more I thought about what was happening to me, the more I knew I wanted to learn about it and to see what doors it would open. That was in February and I started to read everything I could get my hands on about psychic ability, the paranormal and out of body experiences. As I read and learned, strange experiences were happening every day. I'd either see someone who was dead or I'd hear a voice that gave me good advice or answered my questions.

By August, I was in Hawaii on my second spiritual retreat. I knew the moment I landed on the island this was where I needed to be. I was with other people who were psychic or had some other gift and I knew they could help me and not think something was wrong with me.

The next morning set the stage for the whole week. My roommate and I were sitting on the balcony of our hotel room before sunrise. We wanted to watch the sun rise to start our first full day there. As we sat in the semi-darkness, a big black butterfly came flying from around the corner of our balcony and flew around our heads. There were no clear makings on the butterfly. The sun hadn't cleared the horizon but it was light enough to see this wonderful creature clearly.

It flew around my roommates' head and then around mine and started to fly away. We both wanted it to come back so my roommate said, "Let's ask it to come back telepathically."

I agreed and we both sent out thoughts asking the butterfly to come back. It turned around and flew back at us. Then it flew through the closed screen door of our room and disappeared.

Let me explain; the screen door on the sliding glass patio had been closed. We had closed it when we came out to watch the sunrise because we didn't want any bugs or lizards to get in while we were watching the sky. The butterfly flew right through the screen. We both looked at each other in amazement. Where had it gone?

The sun was almost up now and we had plenty of light but the butterfly was nowhere. If it had hit the screen door, we would have heard it or seen it bounce off or something. We looked around and found nothing. We opened the screen door and went into the room but the butterfly was nowhere to be found.

My roommate started to laugh and said, "We've just witnessed a fourth dimensional butterfly. That means there's going to be a lot of transformation for us this week." I wasn't sure what transformations were in the works for us but I was excited to think something was coming my way.

I went back out to the small balcony and looked into the sky. There, just to my left was the most beautiful rainbow I had ever seen, but there wasn't a cloud in the sky and it hadn't rained. I began to understand that this new world I was being introduced to was going to be a magical one.

I learned so much that week. Every where I went I had a new and different experience. When I returned to the mainland, I wanted to learn more. I felt like a different person and I loved it. I asked the Universe to guide me and show me what I was supposed to do with the rest of my life.

It was only a few weeks later I was lead to a school that helped new psychics. It was just what I had been praying for. I loved it! The other students and teachers treated me as if this gift was as normal as breathing. I felt no pressure and I could ask all kinds of questions and really study the energy system of the human body. I didn't feel out of place anymore.

I went to this school six days a week for the next year. I was like a sponge soaking up water. I learned how to use this wonderful gift I had been given. People could come into the school and get free readings from the psychic students. It was great practice and fun. I learned I was psychic, although I prefer to call myself clairvoyant. The Universe was telling me it was my time. It was time for me, the real me to come forward and meet the real world.

After doing readings on people for a year through the school, I started branching out on my own. For the next 2 years I read people and my business grew. I learned a lot about how energy and the universe works. I studied everything I could get my hands on about telepathy, energy, psychic abilities and everything else in the paranormal and normal worlds. I was on top of the world.

Finally one of my friends said to me, "If you can read people, you can read animals."

I thought about it for a minute. I had always had a pet and was very attached to the animal kingdom but I was unsure about how to "read" an animal. I was hesitant but my friend was insistent. She asked me to go to a dog show with her just to see what I might pick up from the animals. I agreed and found myself right in the middle of over a hundred dogs with owners and trainers that wanted to know what their dog was thinking. It was a lot of pressure and I was very unsure of myself at first but my readings seemed to be right on and I had a great time all weekend talking to the dogs. This was the beginning of my animal communication and readings on animals.

I learned animals communicate in 4 different ways. They use sound, body language, pheromones and telepathy or any combination of the four; which is also the way humans communicate.

I learned telepathy is like electricity – it knows no boundaries and anyone can tune into it. My near-death experience taught me that when I thought a question about what the paramedics were doing to my body; they would answer it as if I had said it aloud. This is how I now talk to my spirit guides and get help from them. Telepathy is a great way to communicate with everyone.

I use this channel of communication to get in touch with the force that is talking through me while I'm writing this book. I know that sounds strange to many of you, but just wait until you get into the contents of the book!

So with all that said, let's begin the journey of "how old are we anyway"?

How old are we anyway?

Everyone wonders about how old our souls are. We have all heard people say, "They must be an old soul"? Or maybe you feel like an old soul. Where would that saying come from if we really believed there was no life after death or if we thought there was no soul?

Well if we could wrap our brains around the real meaning of the word "forever", we might find we are older than this Universe.

Most of us think this universe is the beginning or ending of life, but what if it's just another place we're visiting on our journey thru the never ending continuum of "no time or space"? Are we so egoistical and short minded we really believe nothing existed until we came to Earth? When our sun burns out in another 5 billion years, it will only be the end this universe, not us.

Scientific theories tell us there were hundreds of universes created before this universe. They have turned into black holes millions and billions of years ago when their sun burnt out. Of course this is just a theory but black holes do exist and there is no way we know of right now to really explore what they are or what they hold in their darkness. So what's to say we didn't start there?

I had a minister tell me once that Jesus had stated there has never been a time when there wasn't God or souls. I don't know if he is right but it's an interesting statement. Think about that. It's a pretty deep statement.

Many of the great spiritual teachers believe there has never been a time without a great power. So how old does that make us? Studies of radioactivity of the Earth and sun show our solar system was formed about 4.5 billion years ago.

If that's true, then our whole universe has to be about double that because before the solar system could form, the Milky Way galaxy had to form and it probably took several billion years to do it. One scientific theory is that the oldest star clusters in our universe are about 12 to 15 billion years old.

If you believe we were made, manifested or born (you pick the term you like the best) about the same time God or the creative power said, "Let there be light", then we are at least as old as the starting of the Milky Way, a mere 12 to 15 billion years young. If that's true what were we doing while all this creating in our Universe was going on?

I believe we were either helping create it or we were in a different solar system learning other things. We could have just hung around this solar system watching it grow so we could be part of it when it was ready for us. This probably took billions of years but there is no time in space so it really didn't matter. When we're in our energy body, a day is like a second to us.

So if God created everything in 7 days, was he using spirit time or human time? I think He worked according to spirit time because there were no humans on Earth at that time. There might have been energy bodies helping him but no humans were on Earth back then. I think 7 days in spirit time could be a million years or more to us humans but who knows. So if 7 days is one million years in our time, maybe it took seven million years to perfect Earth after it had cooled down from the explosion that made it in the first place.

However the number 7 seems to come up a lot in the Bible and in our daily lives. Another example of the number seven in the Bible is the story about Jesus casting out seven demons from Mary Magdalene and putting them into swine. These seven demons or deadly sins, as the Bible calls them, where lust, gluttony, greed, laziness, wrath, envy and pride. (Sounds like they need to be cast out of a lot of people these days too. I'm not sure we have enough swine to handle the job though and I think it might be very unfair to put so many pigs through that.) I think this is a great story but is more of a lesson about our ego and the negative traps we can fall into when we are human.

However, because this Universe is run by duality, if there were seven demons there had to be seven good spirits to counter them. The seven spirits I'm referring to are supposed to symbolize the seven horns and seven eyes of the lamb that came to Earth known as Jesus. These spirits are righteousness, justice, grace, life, freedom, glory and love. (We could really use some of these right now in the whole human consciousness!)

I have also heard about some old writings where Jesus said there were seven spirits that helped create this universe and they look after it. Each spirit is responsible for an element on Earth. One is for the water, one for land, one for fire, one for weather, one for the other planets, one for humans, and one for animals.

Is this why the number 7 helps run this universe? We have 7 main charka systems, 7 days in the week, supposedly God make the earth in 7 days, there were 7 demons cast out, there were 7 spirits helping build this universe and there are 7 main openings in our body above the navel which have to do the spiritual energy system. We have 9 openings all together but the two below the navel have to do with all body functions such as elimination of waste and sex. I find it almost ironic that sex and body waste are located in the same area.

What were we thinking when we designed the human body? Having the same places for waste elimination and pleasure has got to make you stop and think about what kind of metaphor the Universe is telling us.

The 7 openings above the navel are 2 eyes, 2 ears, 2 nostrils and one mouth. All of them have more than one use and all can either gather information or give information. How wonderful is that! Dual purpose in a dual universe. Everything in this Universe has to have 2 sides to it. Duality is one of the laws of this Universe and we can't get away from it no matter how hard we try.

I want to tell you something I saw once in meditation. It was a long time ago but it has stayed with me like it was yesterday. This meditation was the catalyst for this book.

In this meditation I was standing in outer space and looking back at Earth. I was standing next to a very tall and powerful being in a long white robe. He was so tall I couldn't see his face and I was holding his hand as if I was a small child. As we stood there looking down on Earth, I heard him ask, "So what would you like to create today?"

It not only scared the hell out of me but it was a very deep remembrance of what I had experienced somewhere in time – and I think many others have experienced this feeling of helping create this Universe too.

I think many of us had to have a hand in creating things on this planet so we would know in our soul how to survive here, just like we have survived on other planets in other solar systems as other kinds of beings.

I think we've all had a hand in creating many of the other universes and solar systems at some time in the past. Think about it – if we didn't have some part in creating this planet, how would we know there are healing herbs, plants and flowers? How would we know that everything we really need is already here? We had to put it here in the first place so throughout time we would know it was here for us to use in whatever way we needed or wanted too.

We have cement to build things with and it just didn't fall from the sky one day. Everything we have ever invented, imagined or manifested has come from what we already have on this planet.

In this universe our lives are run by duality, numbers, time and space. In another universe our lives maybe run by something else we haven't experienced yet. So creating and experiencing is what our souls are all about.

I believe we will always create. We have the DNA of the creative power(s) that made us. Creating is in our blood, so to speak. It's the same principle that's in play about our parents and other relatives. We are part of our parents and our DNA has some of their traits and we will probably develop some of their talents. Since we are part of the creative force that made this universe, we have to create because we have it in our DNA system to create.

This same creative force is still out there creating more universes. And if this force made us, did it make others who live in the other Universes? Science is proving there are thousands of Universes under construction right now. Science also tells us there were hundreds more but they are now only black holes in space because their sun burnt out.

Have you ever really thought about that? Were there beings of some kind living on planets in those universes before it burnt out? What happened to them? What will happen to us when our sun finally burns out? Will that be the end of the human race? Or will there be another universe somewhere in space that will be ready for us to go to?

We find it hard to understand there is a massive creative force that never stops creating. We can't seem to grasp this concept. However, we follow in our creators footsteps by creating things every second of everyday. We create our own jobs, we create how each day will turn out just by our attitude about it, and we create our own thoughts and opinions on everything. We create our own experiences every second. We create our own lives with the choices we make and we re-create life over and over again through birth.

We are creating everyday but we take it for granted. If we just get out of bed and say we "did nothing" today, we created a nothing day and still created thoughts throughout that day. Even if we didn't even get out of bed, we still created a day where we just rested.

We can't ever do "nothing" as we have to breathe which creates life. We might even die but even that's creating death and a birth on the other side. We create a lot of things including our beliefs, boundaries, marriages, babies, and every moment of our day.

The following list has some things to think about to help you understand how powerful we really are.

1. What the brain does for or against us –
   a.) Puts energy into ideas that we are focusing on so we can manifest them into reality.
   b.) Brings us the energy or situation we're focusing on.
2. The power of thought to manifest what we want and even what we don't want is very powerful.
3. Emotions are just energy patterns that are controlled by our thought patterns
4. When we change the energy thought pattern in our mind, we change the energy pattern in our aura and our body.
5. We need to change our thoughts so we can change our energy and change our lives.
6. When we put thoughts out about the things we want, we do get them back but many of us have closed the door on the returning opportunities from the Universe because we expect to get things in a certain way. The universe will bring us want we need in the way we need it.
7. All the negative thoughts we think can and do hurt someone or ourselves.

8. Be aware of the intention behind your thoughts.
9. Make life an adventure, not a drama.
10. Start being aware of your thoughts so you can control them
11. Never underestimate the power of thought
12. Remember what you focus on is what you will bring to you
13. Thoughts of love and blessings will bring you more miracles than you ever expected
14. Take the first step toward what you want to manifest.

The above list brings with it the meaning of "free will" or choices and what we can do to change our lives in this Universe. This "free will" or the choices we make can be good or they can get us into a lot of trouble.

If we start to look back at the way things have happened here on Earth, I really believe there a general, master plan with a lot of "choices" thrown in to make life interesting. My belief system tells me that as humans or any beings, we can't fail. We have set ourselves up for success; we just don't see it.

We can choose anything we want and never fail but being human makes it more of a challenge to get things done. We are part of the creative spirit that runs all creation here and in hundreds of universes which means we have that ability too. We are very powerful beings, we just don't remember because of the trauma of birth. That's one thing us humans have to work on; retaining more soul memory when we are born.

Soul memory is where our memories are stored when our body dies. Because our brain dies too, our soul has recorded our memories in energy. They are implanted on our soul in a kind of energy video recording.

Human bodies are not pure energy so each time we come back, we need to be reminded about what we are here for and who we really are. Humans need to come up with a way to retain past knowledge so we can make faster headway to the next level of creation and manifestation. I think we're starting to evolve toward this at a faster pace than ever before. Many children being born today are remembering why they came here and even what they were in their past life. With this memory they are focusing their "free will" on choices that will advance them on their purpose and path in life much more quickly than in past generations.

These new generations haven't lost sight of the fact that we are all still connected. Did you know you share 50% of your DNA with a banana? You share 85% with dogs, 95% with chimps, 98% with every other human being on Earth and 99% with your parents. Only identical twins share 100% of the same DNA. (This information is taken from www.thingsyoudontneedtoknow.com)

I know that sounds weird so let me try to explain it. We do have 100% human DNA but the DNA we share with our parents makes us have some of their traits. The strand of DNA that makes us each different individuals is what I'm taking about here. If we shared 100% of that strand with our parents, we'd look just like our parents – we'd be their twin. So the 99% we share with them is only one strand. Some other strands we share with dogs, bananas, chimps and other humans.

The 2% of our DNA we don't share with everyone else is what's makes us individuals. I don't mean that we aren't all human and have the same DNA pattern because we do. But we all have different hair color, eyes, skin color and things like that. That's the part of our DNA that's different. It's like tulips. All tulips have the same DNA which tells them they are tulips however there is a strand that tells them what color they are going to be and any other individual traits.

As we continue to look more into our DNA structure, I'm sure we'll be even more amazed at what it does and how we can change it. It will also prove more and more that we're all part of the same whole or Oneness who created us in the first place.

Maybe the following example will help you visualize how we are all still connected even when we are in the human form.

I'd like you to look at yourself as you would look at a single cell of your body. We all have billions of cells inside and outside our body and each one is very important to the whole body. Each cell has a function and a purpose. Most of the time our cells know what to do to help the body stay healthy however, sometimes a cell gets confused or does things that aren't natural for it to do. Sometimes a cell seems to lose touch with the body and goes off on its' own, forgetting that without the body, it can't survive.

This is how many of us live our lives. We feel disconnected from everything and try to survive without connecting to our Higher self, the god of our heart, the Oneness of the Universe, or to others. This is because most of us can't see the energy connections we have with the Universe and each other when we're in human form.

We only see our bodies but the bodies don't seem to be connected to others, so we forget we're all part of the Oneness that first made us. We forget that without each other, we would be lost in many ways.

If our cells did this or thought this way, our body would have fallen into a hundred pieces long ago. The majority of our cells have a built in "knowing". It's the blueprint of our cells known as RNA. They know they're not only part of our body but if you really look at it, joined together, they are the body. Just like these cells, each human makes up a cell of the Creator that made us.

Each human, animal, tree and living thing is part of a greater whole, a greater body and purpose. Everything that has cells or atoms is part of a larger body that is working together to make the Oneness healthier and better. That makes all of us part of something greater than ourselves. Just like our cells, each one of us is small but together we are the whole.

Let's walk thru the following example as if we were a cell in the human body. Have some fun with this and really think about it.

When a cell is born, it's only a cell that has divided to form another cell just like its self. This new cell has a life and function of its own but it still came from and is part of the cell it divided from; it has the same DNA. Much like we get our DNA from our parents but we are individuals and still part of the human race and have a human consciousness.

The DNA in every cell is the blueprint that tells the cell what it's suppose to do. It's the map of purpose. We all have our own individual DNA, but each of us has the human DNA too. That DNA connects us. I think it's funny that we can look at a group of animals and understand they are all connected but we can't do it with humans.

When we look at group of dogs, we accept them all as dogs no matter what they look like. We do it with cats, birds and other animals but we don't seem to understand it's that way with humans too. Just because someone has a different skin color or ideas, we think they can't have the same wants and needs we do.

We should look at each human as part of the human race and all humans want the same things; love, joy, peace, happiness. This is how each cell in our body understands its' purpose and function and works with the other cells to create balance.

It's like the cells around the heart work together to keep the heart healthy. The cells of the stomach work together and even through they maybe full of a rough gas that other cells find offensive, they still have their function to help keep the body healthy. This is how our outside world functions too.

Sometimes we don't agree with other people and what they do, but they still have a purpose in this world. Even if we find them offensive or don't like them, they still have a purpose. Without the angry people, could we really learn compassion? Without the hateful people, could we truly learn Love? Without seeing the shadowy, dark side of people, would we ever look for the Light? Without some of our struggles, we would ever feel good about our successes?

There are all kinds of cells in our bodies that work together no matter what. There are cells of different colors that form our skin color or moles. These cells can look different from other cells, but in the body, there is no judgment of how a cell looks, only if it's functioning right to help the whole body.

Even the fat cells aren't judged for holding onto fat. They do this many times to protect the body from starvation or because something we have eaten isn't recognized by the body as healthy so it's stored until the body can find out what it is and what to do with it. And don't we sometimes do this with our lives. We gather knowledge and store it in our brain and subconscious until we decide what we are going to do with it.

No cell in the body is judged for what it does. Each cell knows its job and if a cell isn't doing its' job, then it can be replaced with another cell. The body needs all cells to work together to keep it running right. It's a team. If all humans worked together for one common goal, that goal would manifest very smoothly, as long as ego and emotion didn't get in the way.

I find it amazing that each cell is different, yet each comes from each other; they're connected to each other, even through there is a very thin membrane separating them. They work together no matter what part of the body they come from.

But what happens if a cell does get angry or stops functioning like its' supposed to? The body tries to get rid of it. It's like when we get a pimple. The cell that's infected fills with fluid and infection until it has to explode. Many times this explosion damages or kills the infected cell and others cells that maybe close or connected to it. This isn't a pretty picture but isn't that how we look when we are mad and exploding. Aren't we really infected with anger? And when we act like that, we certainly aren't working together for the betterment of the whole human race. This infection can be anger, hate, revenge, jealously; which creates gossip, hurt, disease and even murder.

When we explode with this infection, it can spread to others, just like the infection from a pimple if it's not washed away. When we're with someone that's angry, mad, upset or always complaining about something, don't we feel it? We can get an upset stomach, a headache, or we can get mad or start complaining about things too.

This is just like a disease in the body that starts from one cell and each cell it touches becomes infected. We can stop this disease by not letting this energy affect us or by showing the other person how positive thinking can change their lives. If we're the healthy cell, we can help make other cells healthy. We can help others see that emotions can be experienced as healthy lessons for us to grow and learn.

When we let emotions control us, we block our natural self and stop working to make the whole body healthy. We start fighting with the natural flow of how a healthy body or cell is designed to function. We stop the healthy growth because we have just taken on something that is not really part of us.

An emotion is not a part of our body unless we take it on and let it take over, like a pimple, infection or cancer. But we can let it go, we can isolate it, we can examine it, we can learn from it because emotions are how we learn but we don't have to let it run or ruin our lives.

A healthy cell needs healthy food to stay that way. We need healthy food and healthy emotions to stay healthy too. Love is a very healthy emotion. Love's vibration is naturally known and recognized by every cell in our body. This is natural because love is where we come from.

We're a big part of a Universal Love which is greater than any one person or cell. When every cell in every body works together in love for the betterment of the whole, miracles happen. This is how cancer is cured, tumors go away on their own and many other things happen to the body to become healthy again because it's working in harmony.

We have the "free will", or choices, to work together or fight each other. Fighting takes more energy and is always in conjunction with an ego problem. Ego's can really get in the way of the truth and make us choose unwise choices. We have to make choices every second of the day and we should learn to make these choices by listening to our higher self, not our ego. None of us really understand just how many choices we have in this world. Our choices can change our lives forever. They can change them for the better or for the worse so be careful what you choose.

If we choose something and it goes (what we judge as) "wrong", we have the "free will" to change it into something else or go a different way.

I once heard a speaker say, "We can't fail. Even though we have total free will, the gods have put into place every scenario that could possibly happen with any choice we make; which leads to more choices and more free will."

WOW! Just try and wrap your head around that one.

Most of the time we forget we're still very connected to the creative power that created us. Once we are out of our energy bodies and into the human body, we can't see the energy cords that are attached to all of us. This makes us feel alone and disconnected from something or someone. So many of us spend most of our lives searching for "that something or someone" that makes us feel connected even if it's just for a short time. It reminds us of home and the connected feeling we have when we're no longer on this planet as a human.

Love is the feeling that spawns positive emotions in our lives, just like fear is the feeling that brings negative emotions to us. I believe this is one reason humans are always looking for love. They want to feel good.

There are only two feelings in this Universe, Love and Fear and all emotions we experience are just derivatives of those two feelings. It's when we let these feelings and emotions get the best of us that others usually see the worst in us. We are not our feelings and emotions. We are spiritual beings experiencing feelings and emotions. If we just experience them like we would a ride on a roller coaster and then walk away from them, we'd be much better off.

However most of us keep hanging on to these emotions. We run them through our head and bodies. We make them bigger than they are and soon they're like a cancer and affect every part of our being. It's like a cancer in the body.

Cancer in the body is caused from cells that have forgotten what their jobs are. You might also compare them to rebellious teens that are out of control and run away. Cancer is a rebellious cell. The human race knows a lot about cancer but many times we can't stop a cancer unless we operate and remove it. Even though the body will naturally try to block it from spreading, sometimes that's not enough. Sometimes the cancer needs to be removed.

Isn't that what we do with criminals? We lock them away from society so they can't hurt anyone or spread their hate and cancer. We either treat these people with medications, keep them locked up or we remove them completely from society, which is a death sentence.

Many humans create a cancer of predigest, judgment and other negative thoughts and energies about ourselves and others. Negative energy is the start of cancer in the human race and can spread to the rest of the body or a group of people. This is the mob mentality. This can cause all types of problems and even death.

So we lock people away hoping that by isolating them, their infection will heal. We hope they can return to society and be healthy again. Sometimes this works and sometimes it doesn't. Sometimes people die before they get healthy again.

Cancer is an ugly word and an ugly disease. Cancer attacks the cells. When it does this, the body stops functioning normally. The healthy cells try to isolate the cancer cells. Sometimes the healthy cells will even turn on the cancer cells to try and kill them.

As cells die naturally, they leave the body or drop away to return to Earth's surface. Just think about how many cells fall onto Mother Earth each day. It's a good thing their microscopic and biodegradable because if they weren't, we'd be waist high in dead cells by now. Many of these cell float in the air to help feed something else or fall to Earth to be used as fertilizer.

Each dead cell has fulfilled its life's path, its purpose, its work is done. It returns to the Earth and is absorbed to help in some other way. The body absorbs millions of dead and dying cells everyday. It accepts them as part of the self, as part of the Oneness. It doesn't look at them as dead cells but uses them as food for other cells and the body. Nothing is wasted.

When we die, our body turns back to dust to help the soil but our soul, the part that doesn't die, goes back to the Oneness to be absorbed into the Light and Love from where we first came.

We take back to the Oneness our experiences and the work we did here on Earth to share with others who are still in the energy bodies. We go back into the place from where we came to bring back knowledge and the food of life to other souls. Only then do we understand we'll of one source and work together to better the Oneness. We go back to be part of the whole, yet we are still individual souls.

Just like the cells of the body, when one dies, another is born to take it's place - to function and fulfill its purpose but to still be part of the Oneness. Even though we can come back in different bodies, in different countries, as different colors and sexes, we still come back to work together for the good of the whole. Just like the cells in our bodies, we're working to grow and learn for the betterment of our individual souls and are only divided by a very thin veil known as the human body.

So what is the master plan? I believe the master plan is simple - we are taken care of no matter what happens. We have everything we need to create, live and learn. What could be simpler? However, most of the time after we create something, we wonder what to do with it, don't we?

Everything we create has a purpose. The plants and trees from the dinosaur age are now oil. So what do you envision plastic might be in a million years? Some people say it will take hundreds or thousands of years for plastic to somehow degrade but what if it's supposed to take that long because plastic will be some kind of fuel in the future? What if in a couple of thousand or even another million years we create a use for all this plastic. After all, we have about 5 billions years left in our sun before it burns out and our Universe becomes a black hole like so many others before it.

Until that day, we'll just keep creating and using what we have here on Earth. Just think about what we've done with the Earth's resources. Steel, bricks, cars, batteries, food, and everything else we've created has always been here in some form. It was all waiting to be created and then see how we would use it with our free will. The really cool part is if we screw things up, Mother Nature will just shake us off and start over. We have stories about her doing this in the past. One of these stories is the floods of Noah and his ark. The human race survived that and I believe it will survive much more that is still to come. It's in the master plan.

This is what I believe the master plan is - we are taken care of no matter what, even when it comes to something we call death.

All the great spiritual teachers have told us we are very powerful beings. So if we are so powerful, why don't we use it more? It's because the shock of re-incarnation makes us forget. We have to go from a very high vibrational energy body into a low solid human body. This lowering of vibrational energy can make us forget things. Also, we don't have a human brain when we are in the energy body so we have to start over with a new brain. Many of the memories that are stored in our energy body have to down load into our new brains at a slower pace. This is why we start to remember things at different times of our lives.

So how old are we? Let's just say for fun, there were 100 thousand solar systems and universes older than ours that are now black holes in space. Let's say each one had a lifetime of 20 billion years; which is another theory about what a normal life time for a universe might be.

If we were created about the same time the first universe was created, that would be 100,000 multiplied by 20 billion which equals about 2 quadrillion years.

Now I don't think all of us have been in, on or around all the 100,000 past solar systems but I do think all of us have visited or lived or experienced part of some of them before they turned into black holes.

I think we lived, but not as humanoids, on other planets and knew there were other beings in outer space just like we believe there are other beings now. No one really knows why we feel there are other beings that come to visit, but most of us just feel there are. Where do these feelings or knowing come from? How could we know or feel it if it didn't exist in some form of memory or experience?

Where would all those ideas about outer space visitors come from if some of it wasn't true? Where would we get the ideas for the star wars movies and the star trek adventures and all the cool technology they have? It has to be stored some place in our memories for us to manifest it into reality just like creating plastic or refining fossil fuel. What made us think of these things? Are they awakened in each generation of humans at a certain time? Is this part of the master plan?

I don't know or even pretend to know all the answers but I do know we are taken care of and we must always be creating. How we instruct the Universe to care for us and how we create that care is guided by our own free will. We are the only ones who determine how we create everything in our lives.

The really big question is what happens when our sun burns out in about another 5 billion years? I believe the universes that are being created today will be ready for us when this happens. I think there will always be another universe being created for us. Each one will be ready when we are ready to move there.

I'm not saying there is only one universe at a time with beings in it. I think there are millions of universes right now with billions of beings living in them. I think each universe has its own challenges so we can learn and grow as different beings with different energy fields. We might be solid form in some of these Universes or we might just be an energy body – anything's possible.

If you look back at how long humans have been on Earth, a mere 150,000 to 200,000 years, we have a long time to go before we leave this planet but what is time or even space for that matter. Didn't humans make up time and space to help us get organized. However, I think many times they hinder us instead of helping us.

We've had to deal with time and space for so long we can't even imagine what life would be without them.

Time and space runs most peoples' lives. Without them they couldn't set an appointment or even function. But what are time and space besides made up boundaries we have inflicted upon our selves? We can't even imagine what that means. Wow, a lot to think about here. But while we have our brains engaged, let's talk about time and space.

The amazing part about time and space is we're always running out of them but they are a made-up illusion. They're part of the whole illusion of life. How can we run out of something that doesn't really exist except in our own minds? If we live forever, we'll never run out of either time or space.

Before we invented time and space, when the Earth was young and the gravitational pull wasn't as strong as it is now, we were shape shifters – Lemurians. Lemurians were on Earth as far back as 170,000 years ago and maybe longer. Anyone who has studied this culture agrees the Lemurians were more energy than solid form. They came to Earth to experience being physical. Because they were energy, they could go into the sea and experience what it's like being water. They could go into the trees or animals, rocks or air to feel and experience these three dimensional objects and emotions.

As the gravitational pull got stronger, they realized they were getting stuck in these objects. Hence the stories of Pan – the half man, half goat entity. As the pull got stronger and stronger, the Lemurians couldn't shift into many of the objects on Earth. When they did get into an object, they began to get stuck. This is the theory of how they began to turn into solid beings.

Their vibration was being lowered by Earth's atmosphere where the atoms and molecules move at a much slower vibration. This was the start of their fall. This was the start of the human race. Could this be the "fall of the angels" that we hear so much about in the Bible? The Lemurians seemed to just fall from the sky and into the Earth's atmosphere. It must have been great fun until they started getting stuck here. They realized they needed a body of some kind to stay in this gravity filled dimension. Hence, the human body was created and we've been working on it every since.

No one knows for sure what really happened to the Lemurians but many say once they became human, they no longer felt connected to each other or the Universe. They became selfish and fell into the same trap that we all fall into, letting emotions and feelings run our lives. They started living in fear because they could no longer move as freely as they once did. They found they couldn't create as well either because they weren't used to the heaviness of Earth. This fear grew until they separated from each other because of mistrust. We are still living in fear today for the same reasons. The fear of not having enough money, food, and other Earthly possessions is the biggest fear everyone faces.

No one really knows what happened to these nine foot tall creatures with elongated/oval faces and large eyes with vertical pupils but they seemed to just disappear about the same time Atlantis appeared. Some say they went back into space. Some say they were killed by volcanic eruptions. Many spiritual people believe the human Lemurians became Atlantians.

(I need to add that I know it's not a proven fact Atlantis existed but no one thought the city of Troy existed until they found it. We don't know if Atlantis is real or not because we haven't even began to explore the deepest depths of the oceans. For all of you that don't believe in Atlantis, the jury's still out so try to keep an open mind.)

Did you notice the physical description of the Lemurians? Did it remind you of how some of our aliens are described? Many people believe that Lemurians came from Mars, Sirius and the "Pleiades" because their planets were starting to die. The Pleiades are known as comets now but back in the days of Greek mythology, they were known to be the home of the gods. Here the number seven comes in again as there were supposed to be seven daughters of Atlas and Pleione that lived there. There are several stories about this star cluster and the life it was supposed to have. I'm including some of the books and information on the subject if you would like to look it up.

- **Burnham's Celestial Handbook**, Revised & Enlarged Edition, Robert Burnham Jr., 1976, Dover Publications Inc.
- **Star Names: Their Lore and Meaning**, Richard Hinckley Allen, 1899, 1963, Dover reprint *(Note: Allen's text on individual Pleiades stars can be found at <u>Alcyone Systems</u>.)*
- **Star Lore of All Ages**, William Tyler Olcott, 1911, 1931, G. P. Putnam's Sons, New York
- **<u>The Age of Fable</u>**, Thomas Bullfinch, 1942, Heritage Press

- **The Greek Myths**, Robert Graves, 1960, Pelican Books

Some believe Lemurians breathed through their skin and had no lungs. Some think they were more jelly-like and only communicated through mental telepathy.

Many believe they were one sex but each had the masculine and feminine energies in them so they could create. However, as matter grew denser on Earth, the slower vibration helped bring forth two distinct sexes from one being. Is this why we still have both feminine and masculine energies in us even today?

Some people think the Lemurians were egg-laying and had a third eye which is now our pineal gland. I think that might a little far fetched because if they were energy beings with the capability of reproducing by themselves, they would just divide some of their energy to form another being, not lay an egg. An egg is a solid form and at this time they weren't solid so I have to throw that theory to the wind right now.

However if there were two sexes in the same body, could that explain why we're always striving to reunite as one body through sexual intercourse? This is truly the only action here on Earth that brings the feminine and the masculine energies together in a visual sense. Humans need to "see" things to believe and understand them. Knowing we have both of these energies in us in not enough. Do we have to see and experience them to understand creation?

Could it be this simple? Could we make things so hard? When we make the shift from spirit to some kind of solid or even semi-solid being do we forget what we're doing? Do we get so wrapped up in the human body and human condition we can't see how we can create without having to "have someone with us to do." Some people think we are "programmed" or have archetype personalities to learn certain lessons in our lives.

I think we live several different archetypal roles in our lives to learn different lessons. If we were programmed for just one archetypal our whole life, that would be taking away our "free will" and if that happened, there would be no real reason for us to here. Free will is the only way we truly learn.

Does creating come so easy for us we somehow think we are missing something? Is that why we all think we should be doing something else?

In this universe we are supposed to learn about duality, separation, personal power and free will. We may not have these things in another universe so we should be enjoying them now and learning what they are all about before we go on to another universe. We think this Universe is hard but maybe it's one of the easier ones.

I'm also sure that karma in this universe has a lot to do with why we keep coming back. However, this too is in the master plan. The gods know when the time is right we'll heal our karma and move on to possibly another universe that doesn't have karma or duality.

Try to think of a place where everyone works together to create something good and there's no jealousy, back stabbing, credit taking or any other negative emotion. Or maybe there won't be any emotions at all. Maybe that's why we are here, to experience emotions; just for the fun of it.

The more I read about the Lemurians, the more sense it makes to me. If our creator is this powerful energy source, then we have to be a part of that force. And if he/she/they made us in his/her/their image(s), then we should really be energy beings.

It also makes sense we have lived in trees, rocks and animals because we seem to know so much about them. It's like we are bringing the knowledge of our souls forward to help us remember. This way we don't have to start completely over every time we reincarnate. We just have to bring the knowledge of our soul forward and remember.

We start over every time we come back because we have a different body, mind, time and place but the soul never changes. We may act differently in a different body but that's because we have to learn different things in that body. Each body brings with it different experiences and lessons to learn. Being in a body is an amazing adventure all by its self.

So how old are we? My mom, who at the time I'm writing this, is 82 years old, says her body is getting older but her spirit still feels 35 years old. I have asked many older people about this and they all say the same thing – 35. When I cross the veil to talk to disembodied spirits, they are all about 35. I believe our soul never ages or really dies. The soul is who we really are. If the soul needs to be recharged, I believe we just draw in more energy from other sources and continue on; just like when we need food to regenerate our physical bodies.

So if we never die, how old are we? Does it really matter? We live forever and none of us can imagine what that means. Our human brain might be set up to understand this but very few of us tap into that part of the brain. Even fewer of us tap into the knowledge of our souls. If we used more of our brains without analyzing everything to the tenth degree, we would begin to understand more. But maybe we aren't supposed to use more of our brain than we do. Maybe the rest of our brain is for down loading all the memories of our past lives and we need that storage place.

I believe some of the amnesia we suffer at birth is part of the master plan too. If we remembered everything, what would we have to learn on Earth? Unless our whole purpose here is to just experience emotions and duality.

Maybe we aren't supposed to know it all until we cross. Maybe knowing it all would stop us from experiencing emotions and life in a human form. When we cross and return home, we look back on our present life and see what we did. Then we have the free will to come back to redo it, learn what we didn't, experience something new or teach our lessons to someone else.

The master plan is a simple one and we are all part of it. Each of us are finding our own way to create, live, understand ourselves and deal with what we create. The plan is so simple, just be and create and live. However, emotions get in the way and then we create rules on top of them to make us feel safe and we get lost in the B.S. of life and it takes us years to figure anything out.

We can create life in anyway we want and then experience what we created. It's a great plan but we often get in our own way by letting our ego or another person tell us what to do. No one seems to know where the ego comes from or even why we have it other than to experience it. The ego can tell us we are good, great or bad. The ego can lie and we believe this little voice in our heads. We should try to balance our ego and know it can be good for us or it can be bad for us. It takes practice to do this.

We have to learn to listen to our soul instead of our ego. Our soul will never tell us we are great or bad, it will tell us the truth about who we really are and what we are supposed to be doing.

I think our ego might have started out as a part of our conscious self but worked it's way into being a separate voice years ago. This thing we call "ego" can be very powerful and we have to stay on top of it to keep it from building us up too much or tearing us down completely. Sometimes there seems to be no in-between. That's where practice helps to keep it under control.

Could ego be the devil we hear so much about? I personally don't believe in the devil. I do believe in dark entities and other things that have decided to live on the dark side but I don't think God and the devil do battle for our souls. God's too busy creating to fool around with something as trivial as that. He knows we have free will. He knows we go into battle with ourselves all the time before coming up with a final decision on what we want to do, so he doesn't have to do a thing.

There are no lost souls – just misguided ones and I think eventually even they come back into the Light. It just might take them a few thousand years, but that's their choice.

When I say we were given free will, no one can step in to change our minds if we don't want them too and that includes angels, spirit guides and even the creative power that gave us that will. I believe it's our ego which makes us do so many nasty deeds and we need someone else to blame. You know, "the devil made me to it".

I guess if we didn't have an ego we couldn't learn to ignore it and then we wouldn't be humans here learning lessons on this planet in this universe. There is a purpose for everything, even if we don't understand it. So the ego, like everything else, must be part of the master plan as well because there is a reason and place for everything in this world. There is nothing here on Earth that isn't included in the master plan in some way.

We are now going into the next chapter about life and death. The words, "life and death" are only names we've put on the way we transcend from one dimension to another. They really have nothing to do with life or death.

Life and death can't mean anything if we live forever and continue from here on to something else. Life is just a word as death is just a word. We are here now and there later. We are human now and energy later. Then we go from energy to something else.

We really never age because age is a human term and condition. The soul is not human so it doesn't experience age expect through the human body. Think about all we experience. A soul couldn't experience these things unless it was riding around in a carbon based unit known as the human body. So when someone tells you to act your age, ask them if they mean the billions of years you've been floating around space or the years you have been on Earth this life time. It might just stop them in their tracks and give them something to think about.

Now that I have you thinking, let's go one step farther into something we like to call life or death.

Life and Death –
what's this all about?

Many people wonder about death and they call everyone who is on the other side, dead. Well in my line of work, I like to call them disembodied spirits. They aren't dead; in fact they might be more alive than we are. They've just ended their contract here on Earth and have gone home.

I like to look at this transition in the following manner. We decided to take a long trip to a new place. We spend several days or maybe even weeks putting all the details together of what we're going to do and see while we're there. We make a wonderful to do list and get all excited about it. Most of the time this "to do list" has so many things on it, we don't have time to see them all. Sometimes unexpected events happen and we get side tracked and never get to see what we really wanted to see because we ran out of time.

Then all too soon, it's time to go. We get back into our car and make the trip home. When we get home and look back on our trip, it seems it was too short and we never accomplished what we wanted to do. We had fun and did many things but never got to "do it all" but we are now home and it feels good. We unpack our bags and put the souvenirs on the shelf to remind us of what we did. This is life and death.

We make our contract on the other side, home as I like to call it, and get ready to come to Earth to learn things. When the time is right, we incarnate into human form and start our journey. When we are finished, we get out of the body and return home to remember everything we learned while on Earth.

Leaving the human body is like stepping out of a cement mixing truck after a long hard day and putting on a jet pack to fly home in. Wow, what a freeing experience. When we go back to our energy bodies it's like we've been wearing cloths that are too tight and our soul is finally free of them. We can breath again, travel wherever we want to go and know we live forever.

We don't remember we live forever when we're in the human body because death and birth are very traumatic to the spiritual soul and our energy system. The vibrational shift we have to do in both cases is amazing. It takes a lot of energy to be born because we have to lower our vibration to fit into the heaviness of the human body. In the same aspect, to die means we have to raise our energy vibration again to join the spirit world.

Remember the near death experience I told you about at the beginning of the book, well, it taught me a lot about life and death very quickly. When I realized they were going to use the paddles on my chest, I made a choice not to have that happen. It seemed I knew I could come back into my body. All I had to do was make a choice to do so.

Somewhere in that unconscious state of consciousness I was in, I remembered the horror stories I had heard about the bruises they leave on your chest and I wanted no part of that. I have to say, I'm an Aries and we don't like to have bruises or even look bad, so this might have brought me back into my body more than the thought of death. Death didn't bother me at the time, but being bruised did!

I had to know that getting bruises on my chest were somehow worse than dying. I know that sounds strange but that was what I was thinking at the time. The only place I could have had that thought stored would have been in my energy body because at the time, my human brain was shutting down. I was unconscious so my brain couldn't have been thinking. Every time I remember this life changing event, I remember all I had to do was to think something and I got an answer. I know this is how I communicate now with animals and loved ones who have crossed.

The only difference between being alive and dead is a solid form we call a body. When we're out of the body, we're still living and very much alive. We're just in a different form.

When my dad was in the final stages of his life, he used to look at the end of his bed and talk to his father, who has been "dead" for over 50 years. He would talk to him about many things and then go off to sleep. Once he asked my mom why there were so many dogs in the hallway at the rest home. Of course, my mom couldn't see them and wondered what he was talking about. I know he was seeing the deceased pets of many of the other patients who were sitting in their wheelchairs in the hallway.

I wondered if any of these other people saw or felt their wonderful pets near them. It was a great vision for my dad and for me. It provided even more proof to me that our pets don't "die" either. They stay around us and wait for us to join them on the other side.

My near death experience and then watching what my dad went through as he prepared to cross, confirmed to me that there is so much more to life than just being human. I'm sure there is no death, only a transformation.

As I've said earlier, it was soon after I returned home from the hospital after my near death experience that I realized I had changed. Besides seeing images of people on my walls and ceilings, I felt like I was never alone.

I had been taken to the edge of death's door and I now realized how close it was. It seemed like it was only inches from the world of the living. Death is a very thin veil where everything can be heard and seen. It's a place we can think about something and either get an answer or create it. It's all done by just thinking it.

I learned there was a loving force on the other side of this veil that can't be described or felt to its fullest on this side. I learned the Universe had given me a great gift and then brought people into my life to help me understand this gift.

It seemed all I had to do was ask and someone came into my life to explain something or guide me in the direction I needed to go. It seemed people would just show up and things would happen for me. It was wonderful and scary.

I learned about our body's energy system and how it helps control this gift I now have. I was reading everything I could get my hands on about psychics, energy, charkas, the soul and everything in between.

I studied and worked and some of my friends asked me to do "readings" for them. It was great practice. I was always surprised at what I knew about the people who sat in front of me. They would ask me questions and the answer would just come out of my mouth. It was a wonderful feeling being able to help others with their troubles or uncertainties. It seemed whatever I said to them settled their fears and made them look at life in a different way.

This was the beginning of getting in touch with people on the other side, the people we call dead. I started talking to the shadows and heads I saw on the walls of my home and other places. I sometimes found they had messages for me and sometimes they didn't. I loved talking to these spirits as they always seemed to know something about what I was learning. They were like teachers to me and still are. Even to this day I talk to them more than I talk to people in the human world.

There's a lot to say about death and birth but this is the important thing to remember; the shock of dying is the same as being born. Many times people will tell me their wife or husband made an oath to get a message to them from the other side. They'll ask me what "their" secret word "is"; as if they're testing me to make sure I'm talking to the right person. Well here's the answer to that question – most people don't remember what the word was because of the trauma of death.

It's like asking a new born baby to remember why they wanted to be born. So don't expect any soul to remember what you remember because many times it just doesn't happen. Remember we leave the human brain behind too. We really leave all our humanness behind so we don't remember everything. We remember what we need to remember.

Life and death are the two biggest things we can go through and we do it many, many times. I've been told I've been here 38 times and this is my last time here. Edgar Cayce said you had to be here at least 30 just to get the hang of being human. Many of us do 100 or more lives. Some do less, that's part of our free will and the choices we can make.

When we're in spirit or energy form, our energy vibration is very high. When we're in human form, our vibration is very low. When our mothers are pregnant with us, we go in and out of the body during that nine month pregnancy. The soul very seldom enters the body before we are actually born. The fetus grows and the soul visits the body. This way the soul can get used to the lower vibration of the human body. This allows the soul to slowly lower its vibration to match that of the body it's going to enter. By the time the human baby is born, the soul has lowered its' vibration enough to enter the body without damaging it.

When we die, our energy vibration has to go back into spirit or a non-human form so we have to raise our vibration very quickly. This is also hard on the soul and we do forget some of things we did over here. When we're in spirit, nothing material means anything to us. We can't touch it, use it nor is it really important. We see all things as just objects created by our human minds.

We still check in on our loved ones but what was important when we were in the human body just isn't important anymore. What we did and learned are important! Trying to remember everything we said we would do when we die is like saying we'll remember everything we want to learn when we're born. So if a psychic or medium can't come up with the "magic word" you want to hear, it really doesn't mean anything.

After our loved ones are on the other side, we have this deep want to get in touch with them. We want to know how they are doing, what they are doing and if they miss us as much as we miss them. Somewhere deep inside we know we can contact them but fear holds many of us back from doing it.

The best way for anyone to get hold of their loved ones on the other side, is to look, listen and understand. When your loved one wants to get in touch with you, they'll flicker a light or maybe move something. They can touch you or blow on you but to materialize into a solid form is like you trying to disappear. You could do it if you really wanted to and practiced it long enough but it would take a lot of energy. So don't expect your loved ones to just "show up" in a solid form whenever you ask them too.

Seeing our loved ones in a dream is easy because we are meeting them on their level. We have come out of our body and are traveling in the fourth dimension. We keep our energy vibration in check because we are still attached to our bodies but we can do a lot of things in the 4th dimension. We are actually with our loved ones and can think thoughts to them. Many of us try to talk in dreams and we wake up. Next time you're in this dream state, think something to the person you are with and see if you can't get their thoughts back.

If you can't remember your dreams or you think you never see your loved ones in your dreams, they might show up as energy when you're awake. This is the cloud we see out of the corner of our eye or a feeling we get that they are with us. If you look carefully, you can see signs and messages they're sending you but don't ask for sign after sign after sign. It just won't happen that way most of the time.

If you can't seem to get the connection, then call a person like me. We can tell you what your loved ones are doing. Many times we can tell you what they are saying to you or if they have any advise for you. Many of us can even help you hear your loved ones. Death is only a very thin veil away. (I hate the word death – I like to say life after life.)

I'd like to take a moment here to answer some of the most asked questions about life after life. First, everyone has free will and we can die anytime we want. If you were to study sheep, you'd learn a sheep can get up in the morning and think it's a good day to die and just lie down and die. There is nothing wrong with the sheep other than he wanted to die. What's even a stranger thing is if the sheep herder doesn't remove his body right away, the whole flock might just follow what the one dead sheep did. Then you would have lost the herd just because one sheep wanted to die. It's hard to believe but it true and we can do it too if we really wanted.

(Also, we think sheep are dumb but did you know a sheep can remember 50 different faces for up to 5 years?

Just a little known interesting fact I thought I'd throw in. Go to www.nature.com for details and more studies on sheep and how smart they really are.)

What I've learned from my readings throughout the years is we all have about five times in each lifetime we can choose to die or not to die. I don't mean suicide either. I mean times when we thought we might die or there was a chance we could die but didn't. Somewhere in our consciousness we know we can manifest death as well as life. It's just a matter of knowing which we want at the time. I can remember several times when I could have called it quits and died but didn't. The following are a couple of examples of what I've experienced and maybe they will help you think about your life and if you have ever been near death but decided not to die.

When I was four, my family was spending a couple of days at the beach on the Oregon coast. My older brother and sister had walked me down to the edge of the ocean with instructions from my parents not to let go of my hands. Well, if any of you are familiar with the waves on the Oregon coast, you know they are unpredictable and the seventh wave in any ocean is always a big one. (Here's that number 7 again.)

When my siblings saw the seventh wave coming, they dropped my hands, turned and started running back to my parents. I turned to see where they were going and the wave hit me in the back with the cold icy fingers of death. It grabbed me and I went face down in the sand and was being pulled out to sea.

My parents saw what was happening and my dad drove into the ocean, even though he didn't know how to swim. I don't remember how he pulled me out but I was wet and had sand wedged in and around every part of my body. I was coughing and chocking but after a few minutes, I stopped spitting out the salting water and started breathing again.

Another time was when I found out I had cancer. I was 25 years old. The cancer had been caught early and I somehow knew by just removing it, it would be gone. I started living my life in a new way and mentally made the decision to stay cancer free – it's worked for the last 30 years.

I also feel my near death experience with the Aspartame was another time I could have walked the rainbow bridge home but I didn't. I feel if I would have said, "Its okay, I'm ready to stay here in this white cloud of love and peace and I don't want to go back to my body," it would have been fine and I would have stayed on the other side.

So think about how many times you might have been able to say good bye but something in you just wasn't ready to leave this planet.

People ask me all the time about the babies who are still born or die shortly after birth or of crib death? We usually blame God for not protecting them but even a little baby has an old soul with free will. Some souls come back for a short time to learn or experience what they want or need too. Maybe a baby needs to experience death as a baby to fulfill a contract we're unaware of.

I've done readings on souls where the body was still born and the parents are wondering why or if they did something wrong. In many of these cases the soul has told me they just changed their minds. When they started to get into the body, they decided the time wasn't right or they didn't want to come into the body after all. This is how much free will we have.

God, the Universe, angels, whatever your belief system is, will never interfere with your free will because it is a gift to everything on the planet. The rulers in heaven all know we can't fail nor can we really be hurt. When we "die", we return to our energy body with more knowledge for our own understanding. I always tell people that even the angels won't stop you if you really want to jump off a 40 story building. However, on the way down they will whisper in your ear, "Not a wise choice" but they'll never leave your side. They hang in there with you all the down and they might even grab your soul before you hit and take you home; which will save you a lot of pain.

So take a minute to think about events in your life and see if you can't come up with a time or two when you may have decided to stay here instead of dying. Be grateful you decided to stay too. Living as long as we can is something we should all try to do because the longer you live, the more you can experience. Most days we really don't think about life or death until someone dies. Then it hits us. We don't really think about a birth in the same way because we know it's the beginning of a life, well death is the beginning of life on the other side again and should celebrated as well.

Many of us get so busy with life we really don't think about anything else and that's okay but we forget to get in touch with other family members or friends when we get too busy. Then someone dies and we feel badly. We wish we would have talked to them more or seen them more often. We wish we would have at least called them on the phone. We don't think about life or death until it happens to someone else, then we want to connect to everyone we haven't talked to in years.

Those of you who have children know they grow up and leave home and we don't hear from them everyday. This is a normal thing in our society. It's called being on your own or growing up. This is how we all learn about life and ourselves.

It seems the, now grown up, kids only call when they need something. Don't we do this to the creative power we call God? When we leave the spirit world to come to Earth, we are growing and learning. We don't think we need to "call home" everyday. Some of us do "call home" by praying or meditating or other spiritual activities but many people just forget about the connection to the spirit world and that's okay. There's no judgment on us if we forget to pray everyday or even if we only do it once a year at church. The other side doesn't judge us.

Our creator knows how busy we make ourselves down here and just smiles. After all, we are doing what we are supposed to be doing, creating, living and learning. This creative energy, God/Goddess or whatever you would like to call it, gave us spirit guides, angels, helpers, teachers and many other entities to help us along our path in this life time.

These spirits are with us for several reasons. 1. – to help us with our lessons and give us support. 2. – to help us keep our connection to home. 3. – to remind us there is no death.

We should look at death as life, just in a different form. After all, we're really more comfortable in our energy body then in the human body. In the energy body or Spirit, we have no pain or other physical problems. Our soul still lives and we still have many of the same qualities we had when we were in human form but we understand more about why we chose to become human in the first place.

As I've stated before, when we incarnated into the human body, the soul has to lower its energy vibration. Because our bodies are carbine based and heavier than energy bodies, we have to slow down our vibration. If we didn't, we would explode the body and that wouldn't be a good thing.

There is another saying I'd like to bring up about the body and what we say at funerals. Someone usually says something about the body returning to the Earth from where it came. Because our body was made here and has many of the same elements the Earth does, it has to return to the Earth. It's too heavy to go into the spirit world of energy.

When we die, we all lose weight. Some people say this is the soul leaving the body and some say it's the last breath of air leaving the lungs. It has never been proven that it's our soul but if everyone losing about the same amount of weight, what else could it be? Not everyone takes in the same amount of air or loses the same amount of fluids at the moment of death. Just something to think about.

In death the body has to stay here. It's vibration is so low it can't join the spirit world and once the soul leaves the body, its' purpose is finished anyway. There is no more "life" in the body. We think our body is life but it's our soul that gives life to our body. The body doesn't give life to the soul other than carrying it around. The body is only a vehicle for our soul.

When the soul leaves the body, it has to return to the spirit world because that's were it was created. The old saying, "as above, so below" is greater than we think. Remember this is a universe of duality. If the body stays here, then there has to be an equal reaction to something going away; which is our soul. So everything that happens "above" has to happen "below" in some form and visa versa.

After we're born, the soul has the choice to either enter the body or stay in the spirit world. Like I've stated, this is why we sometimes have babies that die within a few hours of birth. Our human brain can not understand this. We think everyone should live or fight to survive but we all have different contracts and no one really knows what someone else has come here to experience. Free will is an amazing gift and we don't even understand the half of it.

We're wired with survival DNA and to think someone might not want to be human is beyond our understanding. Many times a spirit only has to enter a human body to finish a lesson or heal karma and then they return home again. None of us knows for sure what another soul has to do here on Earth to achieve their lessons.

When we're born, our parents and other family members greet us. We usually have contracts with these people for this lifetime. These contracts are made in the spirit world many years before we reincarnate. These contracts can be anything from agreeing to be your parents and raising you, or giving you away at birth so you can find the right person to teach you what you came here to learn.

Many times we don't remember our contracts because the trauma of birth makes us forget, just like the trauma of death. However the Universe gives us reminders and messages throughout our lives as to why we're here, if we just listen to them. Our life lessons never go away but with free will we can change how we want to learn them from moment to moment with the choices we make.

The master plan is one of learning to experience and enjoy but some of us choose to learn our lessons the hard way with drugs, alcohol and other harmful behaviors. But never judge anyone's path because some of us came here to experience these things too. A homeless drunk might be working through his contract exactly as planned. So judging someone is better left to the Gods or at least to someone who knows what that person came here to do.

Once we go home, we have a life review to see what we did. We are surrounded by angels and others to give us support as we look back at our lifetime. It's reviewed with no judgment only love. We see what we did and if it was beneficial or destructive. This is how we learn and decide if we want to come back again.

One person may murder another in this lifetime because the person they killed had killed them in another lifetime. It may not make sense to us but then we are just here to experience and learn and many things won't make sense to us. Don't get me wrong, I don't think any murder is right, but I can't judge anyone because I don't know their contract. They might also be learning that murder is not the right choice. Maybe they are learning karma can be healed by energy and thoughts and doesn't have to be healed by actions. Maybe the two people involved in the action of murder had a contract to help each other learn and this was the only way to do it.

Maybe one murder put so much light on the subject it helped heal it for many more people. I believe so much has been brought forward about child abuse because we had to look at it, put light on it and then start to heal it. Many children might have a contract to go through abuse so everyone becomes aware of it. Their contract might be to help get laws passed to stop it. It's been going on for thousands of years and we are just now starting to understand it and deal with it. So maybe some people have contracts about murder that include bringing it to the surface for the betterment of the human race. After all, brothers have been killing each other since the days of Cain and Able.

These are just some of the many things we'll never understand and they really don't matter in the long run. I always tell people if they don't get it, maybe they aren't supposed to get in this lifetime. We won't understand everyone else's life contract or what they came here to learn and experience. We won't understand everyone else's actions or words or thoughts. The best we can do is to make sure we understand ourselves. Get to know your contract, who you are and why you are here and work toward fulfilling it so you don't have to come back and try it again.

This is what life on Earth is all about. It has taken us a lot of forgetting and then remembering to figure out Earth is just another stop along the way of creation and learning. Life and the crossing to go home, or death as some people call, it are just part of this creation.

The only thing the creator promised was our souls will last forever. He never said the Earth, the sun, the stars or anything else would last forever, just our souls. So if we can start to look at this statement as the only truth in the Universe, we can start living our lives from a different prospective. We can understand this Universe is just one of many places we can live, learn and experience different things as different beings. We don't have to be afraid or wonder what's next. We can live for today and know tomorrow is already taken care of – no matter what happens.

It's like we know and expect the sun will and does raise everyday. How do we know this? Or are we so used to it, we just take it for granted? We also know the sun will go away at night so we can rest. We don't worry or even question it and most of the time we don't even think about it. But who set that sequence of events in motion so it would happen every day and night for billions of years?

We don't worry about summer not coming or the moon will never shine again. We take it for granted everything will work the same way every day. That means everything on Earth has to be taken on just blind faith. We have no promise or guarantee that the sun will shine tomorrow. Somehow we just know it will happen over and over and over again.

So why is being born, living a life and then dying and having it happen over and over again so hard to understand. I believe every external movement, event, happening, etc. has something to show us about how we are made, why we are here and what really happens to everything in this Universe.

Understanding and knowing this can take a lot of stress off our shoulders. I don't remember our creator ever saying, "I'm creating this just to make you miserable!" Whoever or whatever that power is knows we make ourselves miserable enough without his help. Everything was and still is good if we just look at it from a different prospective.

Even death can be a blessing when our bodies decide to start giving out. We choose the body we are in and we choose to have several things happen to us so we could learn from them while we are in this body. We might not be able to change the basic lessons in our contract, but we can change the way we learn them. We have the choice of learning them the hard way or learning them the easy way. You choose which way you want to go by the choices you make every minute.

However, there are rules in this Universe and we all have to play by them. The biggest rule is whatever you do, think or say will come back to you and that's how karma works. So if you have been nasty all your life to people or animals, expect it will come back to you for awhile even after you've changed your ways. It's just a healing that has to run its course.

This of course doesn't mean you are going to hell when you die either. I don't believe in Hell. I believe it was made up by some egoistical priests who wanted control of people and needed something to scare the crap out of them.

We are our own devils and we create our own demons. Now I know there are dark entities out there as well as Light ones, remember duality. These dark beings have just as much free will as everyone else so they can stay in the dark as long as they want. They can also decide at any time to go into the Light and become a whole spiritual being again.

Even dark souls have angels around them just waiting for them to ask for help. If they don't, then the angels just wait. After all, forever is a long time. Even if these dark souls don't go into the Light before the Universe collapses, it's okay. Somewhere down the forever road of time, they will change their minds and see the Light.

Dark souls can be in the human third dimension or in the spirit 4th, 5th and 6th dimensions. However, the higher dimensions have more light and dark entities don't like light. The more light they get into, the more they either run from it or decide to join it.

The best way I can describe these dimensions are different energy vibrations. With each dimension comes more Light and with more Light comes a higher vibration. Dark souls have a lower vibration because of the dark energy they carry. They allow themselves to get caught up in physical attachments which add to their slower vibration.

Being human is experiencing life in a different dimension, just as death is experiencing life in a different dimension. If we can understand we are spiritual energy beings having a human experience, we can start to see how and why we are here. If we can also understand that death is nothing more than moving from one form of a body back to a form that we started from, we can allow death to be okay.

If we are billions and trillions of years old, why fear death? Every civilization on Earth has recorded or wrote about an after life. Why did they write about it and were did those stories or thoughts come from? It wasn't a new concept that Christianity came up with! It has been around long before the coming of Christ.

It's a cycle we go through just like the flowers, trees, animals and everything else on Earth. We're no different. We should understand this cycle by now. Don't you think it's in our DNA? Of course it is. We start dying the moment we are born. A flower starts dying the minute it pops thru the dirt.

The cycle is being born; fulfill the life's purpose, die and be reborn. Being an animal communicator I see this all the time. I know many of the souls that were dinosaurs are now our pets. There are stories about animals and how they were actually supposed to be the guardians of Earth. However, when they incarnated, they either forgot or changed their minds, so we came to Earth to help and we became the guardians of the animals and the Earth.

The problem now is we have forgotten what we have come here for and because it has been that way for thousands of generations, we have messed things up pretty good. We have a lot of work to do to get Mother Earth back to the place where she is again balanced and beautiful. If we don't, she will shake us off and start over without us. That's what she's done throughout time and that's what she'll continue to do until our sun gives out.

Which brings me to another point; we're the only species on Earth that questions why we're here or what we're supposed to do while we are here. Dogs don't ask why, they just act like a dog, live their life and when they get old or sick, their DNA tells them to go off and die. They know they are going home so their survival instinct leaves them. They can let go and leave this plane of existence.

Pack animals such as dogs, horses or elephants do off by themselves to die for a couple of reasons. First, they don't want to bring predators to the pack. Second, they want to die quickly and with dignitary. All animals can smell death, sickness, weakness and other pheromones over a mile away and they will search out an easy kill. This is the way of the real animal kingdom.

The real animal kingdom is eat or be eaten. They understand survival and live it everyday. They survive by living in the present moment and making sure they know what is going on around them. They know if they don't, it could mean death in an instant.

Animals live and die just like a flower comes up from the ground, blossoms and dies. It doesn't ask why, it just does it.

If we would just create what we want every day by either thinking it or just doing it, we would understand we are here to experience many things in many different ways. We are also here to learn from other people and experience things through their thoughts and actions.

Have you ever run into someone who seems to have experienced the same things in life you have? It's kind of fun and yet spooky to find someone who has the same amount of kids that have the same birthdays or names. Or maybe you are a member of a cancer survival group or some other organization where everyone has had a similar experience. Why are there so many of us experiencing the same thing? Because each one of us is an individual soul and we experience the same event in a different way. Then we take this experience back home to look at it and see what we learned from it.

If we start to understand the rules in this Universe, we start to understand the "why", the "how" and the "when". We also learn the "why, how and when" aren't all that important. It's the experience that's important. It's the process along the way, not the end result. Why things come to us shouldn't matter. The fact that they do is the important thing. The "how" they get to us isn't important. It's the fact they just get to us that matters. It's not the "when" as much as it's the now. Things get to us as we need them. This is a fact of life and a fact of death.

The one thing I'm sure of is we'll never really die and we'll move on from this Universe to another. However I do have to inject something here before we move to the next chapter. If we believe we'll never die, why is murder, control over someone or other abusive actions so bad? It's bad because it's a violation of one of the rules and I'm not talking about the Ten Commandments. I'm talking about interfering with someone else's free will.

If a greater power or powers than ourselves made us and gave us free will, than what right do we have to take that away from anyone else? We are heading into a new spiritual time when past life karma and even karma we create today can be healed by energy work, prayer and other thought processes instead of actions. The sooner we understand this and honor everyone's path, no matter what it is, the sooner we can move on with our own life.

But what if we can't move on until the whole group of humans we are connected to, in this case everyone on planet Earth, is ready to move on. Many people believe we visit different Universes in groups of different souls.

If that's true, one of the rules might be that a group can't move on to the next Universe until everyone in that group has learned their lessons.

This could be one of the reasons we stay in a Universe for billions of years. We could be the class of 13012 but no one will graduate until everyone has learned what they need too. And if they haven't leaned it by that year, maybe we just hang around until they do.

In this Universe we stay in one group and that's one of the reasons we seem to know so many people when we first meet them. We have run into them a million times in the last billion years. However, we need to change groups at some point because we would stop experiences new things with new people – it would be the same old thing over and over again.

That brings up the question as to why we have aliens visiting us. Are they part of the next group our souls will be with? And if so, are they just checking on our progress? Are they finished with their lessons in another Universe and waiting for their next assignment with some of us? Is that why so many of us have meant them, so we will recognize them when we are finished here?

Could it be that those of us who haven't seen any UFO's or aliens aren't supposed to because they won't be part of the next group we'll be with? Maybe some of us are going with another group that can't visit Earth so it's not important we get to see or know them? Maybe there's a group like us – they aren't ready to leave their planet or Universe yet either.

We are going to explore these questions and others in another chapter but it's something to think about.

So life and life after life is all about fulfilling what we are supposed to and experiencing what we can. It's a never ending cycle in this Universe. This cycle is here to give us many chances to do the right thing and move on with our souls. We only have a short 5 billion years before our sun burns out, so we better get with it now.

Seriously, none of us knows for sure what is going to happen because of free will and what Mother Earth might have to do to save herself. We can move forward or go backwards or stop, the choice is ours. This is one of the reasons we all need to walk our path and stay out of the way of others on their path. No two paths are ever the same. They may have some similarities, but even when two different people experience the same thing, it will be experienced in two different ways.

So walk your path. Let everyone else walk theirs. Deal with your own fears, pain, joy, love, loses, and all the rest and let everyone else deal with theirs. Remember everyone is here to live life their way and see how the master plan affects them. We all learn differently, live differently and die differently but none of it is wrong.

Now let's look into the illusions that make life so interesting.

The Illusion

I was never a real Star Trek fan but I did and still do find some of the technology on the shows fascinating. I really loved the parts about the holodecks and what the crew could experience in one. They could program any situation into the computer that they wanted to experience when it was played back. In this way they could fulfill any of their dreams and desires from falling in love to being a superhero. Every time I saw this, I would think about how we can create our lives by just thinking it, taking the steps to program it into our minds and consciousness and then watching it unfold before us.

When a crew member was in the holodecks, they were not influenced by outside events or stimulus. Everything that was happening to them seemed real even to the point of taste, touch and smell. Isn't this what our world is like? Aren't we here to create an illusion and experience that illusion or experience the experience of creating an illusion or to live the illusion and experience what that feels like? I believe we are here to experience these events everyday and we don't think about them. We take life for granted.

Maybe that's why we miss the experience of the "illusion" which is creating something and then seeing beyond the illusion to the real purpose of why we are experiencing it.

We have this illusion about how life is supposed to be but it's strange that each one of us has a different illusion. What does that mean? I think that's proof that nothing's set in stone and life is what each one of us makes it. So each life is an illusion of what that person thinks. This illusion is also what makes our lives so interesting. After all, if everyone saw life in the same way, we would soon be bored.

This illusion is also a creation from our brain and the power it has. So what is all that gray matter, which is stored between our ears, we call a brain. Is it our illusion making machine? How does the brain work? Do we program our brain, which is so much like a computer it's scary, and then project that program out to create what we want?

Of course we do, that's why you always have to be aware of what you are thinking or programming into your brain. We don't realize just how powerful we are with this programming. We are always under-estimating the power of our thoughts and how our brains work. We don't think our thoughts are heard or seen by anyone because they are in our heads but we're wrong.

When we think something, we are creating a form of energy, like electricity. We can't see electricity unless it's in the form of lightening or a spark when you touch someone. The lights we have in our homes are not the electricity but the end result of the electricity just like lightening and a spark. Any kind of light generated by electricity is the end result. This is how our thoughts work. The physical manifestation of a thought is the end result of that thought. We think it and that starts the programming process. Then we have to follow through to bring that energy thought into the physical world. Remember, thoughts are energy with a lighter vibration so we can't see them until we bring their vibration down to a physical level.

Our brain works like electricity. A currant of power goes out of our brain with every thought. This current of power is seen and felt by the Universe and a line of power starts searching the vastness of space looking for a "like current of power." When this power meets a "like current of power", they recognize each others vibration and your current or thought brings the one that it matches back to you.

When we think of Uncle Fred, we already know his vibration and energy pattern. This knowledge is stored in our souls and memory. When we think of him, we are thinking of his life force pattern and vibration. The thought of Uncle Fred comes out of our brain with "Uncle Fred's" vibration that we already know on a subconscious level. The thought travels out of our heads with this vibrational "thought" of Uncle Fred and starts looking for the "like vibration". Our thoughts can go out into this world or even into the universe to search out and find what we're looking for.

When it finds Uncle Fred's vibration or energy, it connects. Because we all have a different vibration to our body's and minds, it can only hook up to the Uncle Fred you are thinking about. You put out a unique energy and it can only hook up to that energy. It's like hooking up 120 volts of electricity with 120 volts. You get a good connection and can do things with it. You can't hook up 120 volt to 240 volt and except it to work.

Because we're all part of the human race and consciousness, we do share some vibrational similarities. These similarities are that fact we are human, just like dogs are dogs and cats are cats and they have their own vibration for that "grouping of animals" However we are individuals and have different thought patterns, body types and other differences which vibrate at different levels and frequencies.

My belief is because we share our DNA with everything here on Earth in some way and the fact that everything here on Earth was made or created here or in this universe, we can read any vibration that comes our way whether it's animals, trees, plants and rocks. This would explain why we pick up on other peoples' thoughts when we really aren't trying. This is why several different people in different places on Earth can come up with the same idea within days of each other.

So if our brain is the power plant, think about what we are doing every time we have a thought. If our thoughts go out into the Universe and look for the same vibration to bring back to us, don't you think we should be more conscious about our thoughts?

When we think negative thoughts all the time, we're creating a negative program and asking the Universe to play it back to us. This is the illusion of life its' self. We can have anything we want and desire if we know how to think it and then put it into action. The key here is action or recognizing when an opportunity comes back to us. Many of us think something will come to us in a certain way and are not open minded enough to see it in a different way.

That's why we need to be conscious of our thoughts and what they are bringing back to us. Everything has some kind of energy behind it and the universe will bring back that same kind of energy unless we learn how to cancel the "stuff" we really don't want. Ever wonder why things happen to you, whether they're good or bad? Watch your thoughts and see what you are putting out there.

Many of us put out thoughts and ideas but then we don't follow through with the rest of the programming or action because we think we can't do it. We think it's too hard or someone might think we're nuts. We think there are too many obstacles in the way. This kind of thinking will never get you any where and stops the program from being played out. It's like not programming all of what you want to experience into the computer so you can play it back. Some of us turn the computer off and expect it to work. Some of us ignore many experience or changes; not acknowledging them doesn't mean they didn't happen. When we do either of these, nothing can really change in our lives. The program is stopped or it's not complete or right for you. So the universe will bring you another change just to see if you are going to respond to it.

This is what I like to call "getting your attention". If we ignore things long enough, they will fall apart. It's like not taking care of your house or your car. We need to take care of our lives and what we are doing or not doing. Then and only then can we make wise choices to change the illusion of the life we are living.

It's like getting a computer and loading it with all the programs you need to get email, write a book, draw or play games then turning it on and just sitting in front of it waiting for it to invite you to do something. Unless you actually type on the keyboard or give the computer instructions about what you want it to do, nothing will happen. You'll get nowhere and there's nothing to see or enjoy. Isn't that how many of us live our lives?

If we imagined for just a moment that everything we see, smell or experience in anyway is just an illusion we have created, we would understand we can change it or end it at any time. All we would have to do is tell the computer, or in this case our mind, to stop running a certain program and start running another one; one we liked and benefited us instead of giving us pain.

I love to tell my clients to think about what they would do with their life if they had all the time and money in the world. What's their passion? What's their dream? Once you have that, you just need to walk toward it and see what happens. Too many of us are held back by the "what ifs". The illusion or perception is either we can't change it or we'll somehow fail.

If we created the life we are living today because of the choices we made in the past, then to change it all we have to do is to create something else. The problem is most of us think someone else created our life. We believe someone got in our way so we couldn't create what we wanted. This is not true.

When we're small, our parents made many of our choices for us and we really do learn from those choices. We learn what we want and don't want in our life. I think we have all said to ourselves, "I'm not going to be like my mother or father!"

But many times we do grow up to be just like them because we don't break away from the choices they made for us many years ago. We get stuck in the illusion that if our parents thought it was good then it must be. We forget to think for ourselves and really should ask ourselves if we want to live the life our parents planned for us or do we want to live our lives in the way we want.

In India there is a cast system that has been in place for thousands of years and people still live by its rules today. The basic rule is – if you are born into a poor family you must stay poor your whole life and if you were born into a rich family you must stay rich. Whatever your family does or how they live, you are expected to do it too. Many people have lived painful and unfulfilled lives because of this belief system and many other belief systems throughout the world.

However there have been some people that break away from the pack and the "beliefs" of others and live what they want to live – this is called changing your mind. It might be scary but in the long run it's well worth it.

I was 48 years old when I had my near death, out-of-body experience and I could have ignored the gift of clairvoyance that was given to me through this experience but I chose to use it and help people. This was a big change for me. I wondered how my own family would react. I kept it a secret from them for almost 2 years. Then one day I couldn't keep it to myself anymore. I didn't know what to expect when I finally came out of the closet about my psychic ability but I knew I had to do it.

My parents thought it was great and had me do some readings for them. My brother and his family love it. My nephews can now see auras and call me when one of their cats goes missing. However my sister thinks I'm nuts and refuses to talk about it or even acknowledge it. Telling my family about my gift was taking a chance but it was well worth it. Even though my sister doesn't believe in it, it's okay. We're still sisters and I honor her opinions and feelings.

After a year into my studies of our energy bodies and learning more about being clairvoyant, I lost a very good job. I was single and had no idea what I was going to do next. I heard my spirit guide tell me to move to a very small town where there were no jobs and I didn't know a single person. What was I thinking? Well, I was being lead by the Universe to move to this place and I did. I was scared to death.

What happened to me after I made this is choice was incredible. After five months of watching, listening and talking to people in the town, I opened my own business. It was a linen business and the farthest thing from doing psychic readings. But the choice I made was to create something to pay my bills and feed me. I did however put out my animal communicator and clairvoyant business cards on the front counter by the cash register so people knew who I was and what I did. This was the choice to let everyone know about my gift and be of service if they needed me.

With these two choices, my psychic business grew right along with my linen business. Even though both were growing, I was bored at night and made the choice to deal Texas hold'em at one of the local bars to help get to know more people. It worked and I soon knew more than half the town.

I learned to oil paint which was a choice to expand my knowledge and find a creative outlet. I learned more about who I was in those 3 short years than I had learned in the last 40. It was a great and sometimes painful experience but I look back on it as one of the best times of my life. I learned so much in the 3 years I lived in that small town, it would fill another book.

So what would have happened if I would have said "no" to my spirit guides and moved to Yuma like I really wanted too instead of the small town in the middle of nowhere? I don't know. I don't know what my life would be like but I know I made the right choice by not going to Yuma at that time and timing is everything. I knew I was being guided by a Higher Power. I knew if I listened and made the choices they were guiding me toward, everything would fall into place and it did. There wasn't a doubt in my mind – well maybe just a small one but I kept moving forward and didn't let it stop me.

I believe when we're on the path we're supposed to be on, things will fall into place and all needs will appear as we need them. This is how I live my life, on the edge of miracles every day. It's exciting and rewarding and a magical, mystical place to be.

When I do feel things aren't going the way they should, I either change them or I ask the Universe for clearer guidance.

I truly believe if you're meant to do something, it will come to you. If you aren't supposed to do it, it will be one struggle after another and nothing will seem to go right.

This is also part of the illusion – the judgment of right or wrong.

If things aren't working well, we judge them as being wrong instead of seeing this is how the Universes tells us we aren't supposed to do it. Many of us will force an issue. We work at it until we complete it but it might have taken all our energy, money and time and when we do come to the end of the project, we really aren't satisfied. If you want to do something but nothing is working right for you, you might want to step back and ask yourself the following questions.

Do I have all the information I need to complete this? Is the timing right? Is my vision too small or too large to start with? Does the Universe have a different way of doing it that might be better?

Before any holo-deck program on the Star Trek ship Enterprise could be played back, it had to be programmed with all the scenarios so nothing the person did would be a surprise to the computer and the programming could respond accordingly. This is just what the Universe does for us. We make up the program, that's the idea we have or what we want to create, and we put it out into the Universe by either thought or action. Then we wait to get a response back from this thought or action. It might not be the response we want but it's always just what we need!

Many times we put limits on the way we want to get something and Universe has a different way it wants to bring it to us. We try to control how things should come to us instead of just letting them come in a way that helps us learn and understand. When we realize we can't control the Universe and its' power, we let go and just enjoy things the way they're brought to us.

Just ask and let the outcome be okay; no matter how it looks, feels or shows up. The Universe will always give us what we need in the way we need it. When you want something and ask for it, be open to however it's brought to you. It might take a year but it will come when we're truly ready to receive it.

When it comes to life and the perception and illusion of what is going on here, everyone has their own opinion and that's what makes life so interesting. We don't have to agree with everyone or even with anyone on any subject but we should honor what others believe. Honoring all walks of life is one way to be open to learning and receiving other miracles. If we can't honor life in all forms, we miss many of the wonders and unusual events of life. Being open and ready to receive is the only way to see all aspects of life as we know it and how as others may view it.

The illusion of life is all around us. Life is born from a small seed or egg, it grows, it fulfills its purpose and then it dies. The illusion is somehow all this happens automatically and without anyone noticing. There seems to be no one in charge. Everything just happens like it's supposed too.

We take life for granted until we're near death. We take the plants, trees, animals and even the air we breathe for granted. We don't notice many things that happen around us everyday. We see bees but don't "watch" them to see how they live their lives. We don't learn from them. Many of us don't notice the seasons changing until one day we notice there are no more leaves on the trees and it appears fall came without warning. Events are unfolding around us every second of the day and we are oblivious to most of them. We miss so much of life and maybe that's why we have to keep coming back.

The power that created us notices everything, from the birth of every soul to the death of a housefly. Everything is under the master plan. The only thing that changes anything is our free will but even that is built into the master plan.

With our free will we can change when we learn a lesson, how we learn a lesson and where we will go with the knowledge of that lesson. How much fun can that be?

Many people think God is running their life. I don't believe this. If he was running our lives, why would he give us free will? That doesn't make sense to me. This has to be part of the illusion someone made up so there would be someone to blame when things go "wrong" in our lives. Many of us need someone to blame instead of taking responsibility for our own thoughts and actions.

God knows what we came here for but how we do it is our business. We are under the illusion that if we just keep breathing, God will bring us what we want. Well that's true and not true. He may bring us things just to get us off our lazy butts so we can start walking our path. Ever heard the saying, "God helps those that help themselves"? Well it's true. Until we start taking the steps in the direction we want to go, no one can help us and that includes our angels and guides.

These guides and angels are always there waiting for us to show them what we want out of life. They're ready to jump in at anytime but we either have to tell them what we want or ask them for help. It's so easy we forget. That's all part of the illusion too.

We think if we ask for too much or want too much we are being greedy or selfish. Well go ahead and ask and see what happens. We can have anything we want. Just be careful what you ask for because it may come to you in a way you weren't expecting it.

It's like asking for a million dollars and having your best friend die and leave you the million dollars in a life insurance policy. Most of us would rather have our friend back, not the money. Look at the important things in life and ask for them.

We should try to see that money is only a symbol of an energy exchange, just like bartering. We give money too much power. Giving something that physical that much power will always end up bringing you some kind of misery because we are spiritual and in the end, physical things mean nothing. The saying, "you can't take it with you" is very true. The only thing you can take with you is you. It's better to have happiness, peace of mind and joy, which are all non-physical things, than to have all the money in the world and be unhappy. If we can walk through our humanness without being attached to anything physical we will find a freedom that's elating! However, this non-attachment is of course a choice and part of our free will.

The illusion we believe is that "free will" only goes so far. God gave us free will so we could do as we want and His promise is he'll never take that away from us. I think as humans, we get so involved in the illusion we create we forget the promises of the Universe. We also forget how the rules of this Universe work. We can't stop karma but we can ask for "grace" in receiving it. By asking for "grace", we're asking that whatever comes to us in blessed. It's a way of recognizing what we have created and taking responsibility for it. If it's bad karma, it will lessen the blow; if it's good karma it will make it better.

There is another theory that karma is based on our actions, not always true. Because our thoughts are so powerful, much of our karma is based on our intention. If we intent to hurt or harm someone by our actions, just thinking it can have negative affects on you. On the other hand, if we have great intentions of helping someone and it turns out poorly, we have not created bad karma. Because the intent behind it was honorable, there is no harm. Not having something go as planned is just a way the universe is telling us it's not suppose to happen. That's all.

Taking responsibility for our actions and thoughts and the intention behind them is a big part of evolution. Understanding we are part of a much bigger picture is evolution. Learning, growing, doing and seeing who we really are is evolution. That's what this planet is all about. If we understand that everything is evolving every minute, we can see the illusion of life is ever changing. What we perceived today may not be what we perceive or even believe tomorrow. This is the way of growth and learning.

Many of us humans can see, hear and feel other dimensions but we write it off as our imagination. Science is starting to prove our 3rd dimension is only the tip of the iceberg, so to speak. When we get into the human form, we tend to forget many things we knew when we were in the spirit world. As we discussed in the last chapter, birth and death are very traumatic events to our souls and we forget many things. The one thing we really never seem to forget is we are more than just human. Somewhere deep inside each of us we know we're more than the image we see in the mirror every morning.

My mother always said she wondered who was looking back at her when she turned 82 and looked in the mirror. She knew it was her body but deep inside she still felt like she was 35 years old. I love this because when I talk with souls who have crossed over, they all say they are about 35 on the other side. You see, the soul doesn't age. It's part of the endless creative power that goes on forever. We can't even begin to understand that.

Another illusion we have is we've never "lived" before. We've been alive for so long, we can't even remember when we weren't alive. We do reincarnate several times so we can experience the illusions of being rich, poor, white, black, red, yellow, man, woman, gay, straight, psychic or not psychic, and many other situations. This is what brings knowledge to our souls and helps us create different things in each different life.

One of my mantras is "I bring the knowledge of my soul forward." This is telling my subconscious to remember everything from all lives and bring forward what is important to use in this lifetime. When you say this enough, it gets into your subconscious and you start to remember things from past lives.

I know that's hard to believe for some of you but how would we know so much and seem to remember things we have never experienced in this life time if we didn't somehow know them or experience them in another lifetime? We somehow know anything we'll ever need will always been here. The illusion many of us hold on to is that there is not enough of something or too much of something or something is in the wrong place. None of this is true. It's supposed to be what it is and where it is and why it is.

We are now coming into an age of understanding that nothing in this Universe lasts forever, not even fossil fuel. We are now developing other fuels that are cleaner and better for us and Mother Earth. So everything is already being taken care of and planned out in a way to make life here on Earth everything it's supposed to be; which brings up even more questions.

Why hasn't Earth been hit with more meteors than it has? We see craters on the moon and other planets from meteors or other flying debris. We know they hit Earth millions of years ago but why not now?

Did you know that Jupiter is one of Earth's major shields for outer space objects? It sits in the Universe at just the right spot to actually protect Earth. The planet is so big that one thousand Earths could fit inside it. The gravitational pull around this enormous planet is more than twice to three times that of Earth. Scientists have watched as meteors and other space debris can crash into the planet and have little or no effect on it.

It sits in a place in the heavens that shields Earth. When a meteor comes close to Jupiter, the gravitational pull will do one of two things. It either brings the space matter into the planets' atmosphere and it crashes on the planets surface or it will sling-shot it around the planet and throw it back into outer space. Now who thought about this and then placed this planet right where it would do the most good?

If we looked at the whole universe like this, just a little at a time, we would see so many "planned" things and events we would know we aren't alone and we can't fail. The master plan is one that does not include failure. You're either supposed to do something or you're not supposed to do it. It's really that simple. We just cloud the truth with all the illusions we build into our lives to justify what we want to justify.

The only thing I would suggest to anyone is to once a week step back from your life and see what is really happening. What choices did you make this week? Where are they going to lead you? Did you get angry at something you couldn't change? Or did you just get angry? What do you want to do to change your life and have you started to make the necessary changes – other than just thinking about them? This is how we build our lives and the illusions around them.

What's really nice about our illusion is we can change it anytime we want too. Because no two people see life in the same way there are billions of different illusions running around the planet. It's like playing in the imaginary Land of Oz when we were younger. As we grow, we forget we can play at this thing called humanness. When we are children, we play and do things we don't even think about. Just think about what you did as a child, when you didn't know any better – would you do even half of them now?

Everyday we can redo our personal illusion of life. Each day when we wake up we can start our day with a positive thought or action or we can start it with negativity and be mad at the world all day. What we need to realize is it's not the world's fault we are in the situation we're in, it's ours. Sometimes the outside influences do have some amount of pressure on what we can do, but if we work with them instead of against them, we can change them. These outside influences are usually put there as a way of learning something and if we look at them this way, we can overcome them.

We also view this plane of existence as the only way we exist. This is also an illusion because we are energy beings and we leave our bodies every night while we sleep. When we come to the realization we are energy beings and will continue on no matter what, we can look at life with all its illusions and perceptions in a different way. We can re-program the computer to play a different game or situation; one we want to experience and live in.

When we reprogram ourselves, lots of new ideas and thoughts come to us. We can view even the harmful things, like plastic, in a different light. What's to say we didn't create plastic as our next fuel in a billion years. All the plastic in the land fills might someday be what fossil fuel is today. We just don't know what the future will hold because of free will.

The other illusion is that everything is set in stone, it's not. We may have made a contract before we re-incarnated but with free will we can change it at any time. We can decide to go home whenever we want too.

Right now, as I write this book, there is a big planetary change going on. The planets in our solar system are supposed to be headed for an alignment they haven't been in for 25,000 years. How do we know this? I'm sure science does it by tracking what the planets have done in the past, but really, how do we know what the planets are going to do and what effect it will have on Earth?

This movement of planets and the pull they have on the Earth has sent fear into a lot of people and have them worried about the future of Earth and human life as we know it. But what's going to happen? No one really knows because we don't have any clear records about what happened the last time and the Universe has changed in the last 25,000 years. So who's to say?

Many of us have already lived through many planetary changes and different planet alignments so it's not a big deal. Some people don't remember and think it's new or different. However the planets have been in motion for billions of years and that motion creates change. Until the Universe turns into a black hole, we will have changes – so we better get used to it. We have all experienced these changes from both the energy plane and the human plane. The people who are on Earth right now may have asked to be here to experience this event and to learn a lesson from it.

None of the lessons we came here to learn are written in stone, because that would take away our free will. Even if we don't learn what we agreed to learn before we were born, it doesn't matter because we have learned something else. We can come back as many times as we want to learn whatever lessons we need or want to learn. Remember the trauma of birth and death sometimes leaves the soul without all the remembrances of a certain life time. Sometimes we need experiences to jolt our memory back to remembering and then we can go on and learn something else.

Don't let the illusion of life get in the way of life it's self.

But if the illusion is humanness, what is the purpose of the illusion? What comes after the illusion? If life is the illusion, does there have to be another source of power creating the illusion?

I believe we are the energy beings who have created a carbon based body to experience things that we can't experience when we are energy beings. So we come into the body, which is just an illusion to the energy body, and eat, smell, touch, feel emotions and many other things we either can't experience in the energy body or that are experienced in a different way.

One of the things we might experience differently when we're in the energy body is sex. As an energy body, sex might be just a touch or exchange of energy, which if you think about it is all sex is in the physical body too. However we might feel more of a vibration than an actual touch when we are in the energy body. A form of eating might be taking in more atoms for energy. A form of rest might be just floating on a cloud.

When we die, or cross over, all we're doing is leaving behind an empty shell that will again return to the Earth from where it came. And if the saying of "as above, so below" is true, when the human body returns to the Earth, the energy body has to return to the place it came from which would be the "Spirit world" as we call it.

There are also other illusions we might consider. Dreams are one of them. Dreams are the illusion of sleep but only for the body. The spirit doesn't need sleep. So when we sleep our spirit is free to travel wherever it wants to go. Our energy bodies can teach, learn and meet other energy bodies every night without our conscious body knowing it.

This is what most people call "astro-travel". I'm sure we can travel anywhere we want in this Universe when we are in our energy bodies and maybe even beyond. There is no stopping energy! When we're in Spirit, who knows where we can go and for what reason. Maybe we are searching for something or someone; which leads us to another illusion – soul mates.

We think we have to be with a soul mate to be happy. We somehow think if we have a "soul mate" it will make us whole. Well we're already whole with just ourselves. A soul mate can't add anything to us except experiences or learning and if you really think about it, we already have the knowledge to do that.

We all have hundreds and thousands of soul mates. Everyone we meet is a potential soul mate so we need to get over the "soul mate" illusion. We need to understand that anyone or thing can be a soul mate. I believe all the people we meet in our lives are already in our life contract for us to meet and learn from. They help us in someway or to learn something. That would make each person we meet a "soul mate" in a small way.

When we have a great connection with someone, we think they must be a soul mate and they will make us whole. We should remember other people are here to do the same thing we are, learn and grow and we might not be a "soul mate" to them. They may need to meet us to remember something but view us as a pain the neck instead of a person they want to be with. This is another big illusion – just because you feel something about someone doesn't mean they feel the same way.

We need other people to remind us of our knowledge and help us learn but we don't need anyone else to make us more whole than we already are. Look inside yourself and you'll find the soul mate you've been searching for. Then you can go into the outside world and understand everyone is a soul mate whether we are friends, lovers, enemies, neighbors or just someone we saw on the street and smiled at.

My best advise is to get over the illusion everyone will like us or we need someone in our life to make us happy.

Another illusion we have is our body is who we are. We are not our body; we are a soul that lives in the body. Our body is meant to be what it is this lifetime so we can experience what we need to experience. We have chosen this body in this life time for a reason. We chose different bodies each life time to experience different things

As you can see, everything on Earth is just like the holodecks on Star Trek. We can create anything we want too and leave it behind, destroy it or change it to fit our life and our needs. We are so powerful, yet we waste that power on greed, jealously, anger, and other negative emotions. We're here to experience emotions, but not to become them.

Ever say, "I'm angry at you"? You are not the anger and should say, "I'm feeling angry at you". There's a big difference. If we were more aware of our words and what we were really creating with them, as they come flying out of our mouths, we would see just how powerful they are and how we believe in what we are saying in some way. Even if you yell at someone in anger and are sorry about it later, look at what you said. There is probably some truth in it somewhere.

Another illusion is we can make someone happy or unhappy. That is not possible! Each person is in control of how they feel by what they think. Only you can determine if you'll be happy or sad, angry or forgiving and all the other emotions we feel. Emotions and feelings are learning tools and we can choose to learn from them or live them, the choice is ours. If we decide to just experience them, we can see what makes us happy or sad and make choices that reflect those feelings.

If we choose to live the emotions we usually become slaves and victims to our emotions and never get out of them. The choice is ours and so are the illusions that surround these emotions.

Change your mind and you change your life. Emotions are illusions that live in our brain. They aren't real, not really. We make them up to express how we are feeling at the time. We can change them in a heartbeat. Emotions are created by our perception of life and how fair we think we are being treated. We put ourselves in the situations that bring up emotions to experience them.

Since we put ourselves in these situations by our choices, we can change them. Sometimes this takes a lot of effort because of the "not so wise choices" we have made in the past. Other times, the change comes within minutes.

Take a minute or even a day to look around your world and see what your illusion is and what you think your reality is. I think if you're really honest about it, you'll find illusion is the name of the game and understanding this will help you create a better life and a different way of looking at everything in that life.

Aliens Among Us – US

As I start to write this chapter, my friend has given me several things to think about. First, not everyone believes in aliens or UFOs. Well, I know that! I'm not here to convince anyone of anything, I'm just thinking out loud. Second, most scientists believe there is life on another planet somewhere in the thousands of universes we are discovering just because of the numbers of probability. Third, he reminded me no proof has ever been found that any aliens have visited us. I was quick to let him know if they were here they are probably more advanced than the human race, after all the human species is a very young species, and they probably wouldn't let us know they were here.

Then he had to bring up Einstein's Theory of Relativity, which scientists have proven over and over again to hold true in our Universe. I argued that it might work in our Universe but it might not work in another universe or even another planet. Everything seems to be frozen when compared to the speed of light and the speed of light is seemly not affected by anything else. You can't make the speed of light go any faster or slower.

The speed of light is just that; the speed of light.

The theory also infers that nothing can move faster than the speed of light, at least not in this universe. So please keep an open mind because as I stated, we are a very young species and with all the stories of aliens passed down from generation to generation, we can't rule their visits out completely.

All I know is most people believe there is someone or something visiting us and we can't explain it. Is it aliens? Is it God? Is it angels? Is it just energy from another solar system that's finally traveled all the way to ours? No one has the answer.

So why do we have such a fascination with aliens and space travel? How would this idea about other life forms from outer space be written about in every culture on the face of the Earth of there wasn't some truth to it? Are we so full of ourselves we think we're the only life forms in over a hundred million universes in "outer space"? What is outer space anyway?

How can we judge what "outer space" is when we don't even know our "inner space"? How far to you think "outer space" goes? Why is it called "space" at all? Will we ever run out of this "outer space" or does it go on forever like we do?

Every universe has its own "outer space". "Outer space" is that space that doesn't seem connected to the universe in any way. But what if all "outer space" is connected to all "inner space"? Wow, too many questions and not enough answers I'd say.

How many different kinds of aliens could there be in this "outer space" theory? Hundreds? Thousands? Millions? Billions? Trillions? How many planets that we hadn't found yet could have some kind of life on it? Funny how Earthlings' can't comprehend these things. Is this why we fear the unknown instead of embracing it?

I was watching a program on TV and it seems we have just discovered a new universe with a sun much like ours. Scientists are looking at it very carefully because there is data which indicated there is a planet on the other side of this sun. Because of what this data is telling them, they think there might be a planet much like Earth; except the planet is stationary which means it doesn't rotate on an axis. How exciting we are finding these new worlds but are we really ready for what they might prove to us.

These other worlds could prove our religions are wrong; our theories about how our planet was made could be very much distorted, our thoughts on how humans came to be could be jeopardized and every other "how did it really happen" theory could be thrown out the window.

I know we aren't ready to meet any aliens that don't look like humans because of our fears. We would want to kill them and take them apart to see what makes them different from us.

A hundred thousand years ago there weren't that many people on Earth. Anyone could have come from anywhere to visit this planet and no one would have seen them. But what if there was a ship of some kind that came to Earth. It would be just like us sending probes out into space to explore now. What if 200,000 years ago aliens came to Earth from a distant galaxy and the life forms stayed here? Then what if a couple of them mated with the life forms that were already here? What if these two species evolved into humans? Just something to think about because there are some people out there who feel this is what happened.

I believe because our bodies are made here on Earth, our bodies are not alien to this planet, but our souls are because they were created somewhere else. Where that other place is, I don't know. However, I feel it wasn't here.

If our souls are pure energy and made of Light, then we can travel anywhere we want too at the speed of light, without a space ship. If our souls are Light, they had to be created at the same time there was enough energy in one place to created pure energy beings from the some source. So if you want to say the "big bang" theory makes sense to you, than you had to be created at the same time the very first universe was forming which could have been trillions and trillions of years ago. That first universe could be a black hole now. It might have stayed a black hole for a billion years until it found another energy source and exploded into another universe.

So if we are pure energy in our true form, than the Lemurians that came here didn't need space ships. If they were pure energy, they didn't need to breathe or eat; they just needed more energy which they could absorb from any passing star. If outer space is trillions and trillions of years old, they could have been floating or traveling at the speed of Light for a few billion years just looking for somewhere to land and experience things. Our bodies now are of this world because we are human with elements of the Earth in these bodies so they have to stay here. But our true selves are about 6 ounces of high vibrational energy which can do anything it wants.

This theory brings us to the edge of explaining ghosts and images of people who are supposed to be dead. If they are energy, they can travel anywhere and do anything at the speed of light or maybe even faster – my friend reminds me we can't move faster than the speed of light – but I remind him that's in this third dimensional world we live in. Ghost, spirit guides and energy beings are not in the third dimension. They are in the fourth and fifth dimensions which we have no real information about so we don't know what they are like or what can happen there.

I know there are aliens among us and many of us are "them". If you really think about it, where would we be have come from if not from outer space. I don't believe we were ever apes. Science is starting to prove there may have been humans back as far as 170,000 years ago or longer who were advanced in things like math, building and communication.

I think the missing link story developed for two very good reasons. One, we couldn't prove anything else at the time, and two, we can't remember where we came from and if that's the case, my theory is just as valid as anyone else's.

I believe all the theories humans have about aliens and outer space are stories that feed a fear without any facts and we're just lying to ourselves. Humans, in general, love to make up stories when they aren't sure of something. Call it speculating, wondering or guessing but the more we tell a tale, the more we believe in it.

Who's to say how many beings are out there, after all, there seems to be very little proof that anyone else exists, but many think they do. I'm reminded by my friend to tread lightly here as nothing has really been proven but nothing has been disproven either, as I keep telling him. We just don't know what is going on in other universes and galaxies. They could be far more advanced or have different rules than what we have in our universe. I personally think there are billions and billions of other beings out there but we are separated for a very good reason – we need to experience things and learn things in our way.

Ever hear the saying, "We are god experiencing ourselves." I'm not sure where I heard it but the more I experience and learn, the more it seems to be true for me. I think we're all god and when we die, we take our experiences back home to share with everyone.

So are we the aliens that keep coming back? Why don't we seem to go to other universes? Well I think we might have a life contract on Earth and we have to stay until that contract is over which could be until the end of the universe. Remember time is not an issue when we're in spirit. Time is something man made up to organize his world. A billion years is like a blink of an eye so the mere 170,000 years we have been human is like one heart beat.

If you believe all the writings and interpretations of past civilizations, the theory is that aliens have been visiting Earth for thousands of years. These stories tell us they've been seen and recorded. These visitors were looked on as gods. They were worshipped and let's face it, if they're that much more advanced back then, they could have wiped us out a long time ago.

Not much is known about the Lemurians or any aliens that might have visited Earth back then. We don't know where they came from, nor do we know where they went. They seemed to fall from the sky. They seem to have been pure energy beings that could shape shift into anything they wanted too. Some stayed because they wanted too while legends say many got stuck here because of the gravitational pull of Earth. Their story remains a mystery and many belief a myth. But as with any myth or legend, there is always some truth in it. There is always something more to look into and wonder about. There is always something to discover. Were they the first aliens here on Earth?

Trying to figure out who the aliens are is like trying to keep an ice cube from melting in 110 degree weather. We really have to let them reveal themselves to us. If they need a space ship to travel in, then they have the technology we are working toward. If they are just energy beings and don't need a space ship then traveling would be easy for them. Remember, 100 years seems like a long time to us because of the physical body but if we have been around for trillions and quadrillions of years, a 200 million light year trip is nothing.

Also if they have the technology to travel in space ships for years in order to get here, then they have the technology to keep us in the dark about whom they are and where they come from. And why would they want to show themselves to us anyway? Humans are still very dangerous animals. We have the mixed energy of a physical body with an energy body. It's not an easy combination to live with. Our human body has physical needs while our energy body has completely different needs. Everyday we are trying to find a balance in our lives. Everyday we wonder "why things happen" and "how come they happen" and we worry about things that will mean nothing in the long run. The only thing that matters is we are learning something; having an experience.

We should try to remember we're spiritual beings having a human experience. Whether there are aliens out in space or walking next to us on the street, it shouldn't matter. Just like the color of our skin shouldn't matter. It's what an entity is doing that matters. When we are in the spirit world, we all look like energy and only our thoughts and ideas are different. Yes, we have thoughts and free will even on the other side.

Here's another thought, if we were all created at the same time, even the beings we call aliens, were created when we were. That means they have to be connected to us in some way because it was the same source that created all of us. And if a "god" made all of us, then we would all be part of that god like we are part of our parents. This should mean we have some of the same attributes of our creator. Was this what Jesus was talking about when he said "you can do so much more." Or when any great teacher said we can do anything we want too because we have the power at our finger tips. Many of the great teachers of Spirit talk about the "god-like power" we all have.

Which brings up another point; if we were all made at the same time and we have been to different solar systems to learn things, why wouldn't we all know the same thing? Why would some beings seem to be more advanced?

If you believe we are each part of "god" and are here to experience events and emotions and take them back home with us, it would explain why we all experience things differently. We are "god looking at things in different ways." It's like having 10 eye witnesses to a crime. Most of the time you will get 10 different accounts of what happened and what the suspect looked like. The only thing they can agree on is there was a crime committed.

We do this to ourselves every day. We analyze everything over and over again in different ways before we take action to see how it could turn out. We want to know the outcome before we take the action – which doesn't work in this universe. We'll truly never know the outcome of an action before we do it because of "free will" and timing. But if we are "god" and we are trying to experience our self, we should just do things to see what happens. Now don't go jumping off a cliff or anything stupid like that, but thinking too much about what we want to do can cause us to miss the timing and then we've lost the opportunity, at least for awhile.

As a medium who talks to people who have crossed, a couple of people on the other side have told me they can travel to other planets but I've never asked them about traveling to other universes. I'm not sure they're allowed to tell me if they can travel that far or even if they remember traveling. Maybe we aren't allowed to know yet. Maybe that's just one of the mysteries of this life.

Why are we so interested in the sky and outer space anyway? The human race has looked to the sky for guidance and gods since the beginning of human time. If there was not some truth to this, why it would have lasted so long? Why would there be this longing to go into space if there wasn't something out there for us?

The other question is, with all our technology why can't we prove where we came from? Why can't we prove there are aliens? Why are there so many unanswered questions?

I think the main reason we have so many unanswered questions is because we need something to explore and learn about.

Have you ever looked up in the sky and felt you had been up there before? Or you feel a longing to somehow be with the stars? The night sky reveals much of what we can't see during the day but the stars are there 24/7. They twinkle and move in the daytime too. Once in awhile if you're lucky and are in the very present moment, you'll see a flash of a star in the daytime. It's quick and rare, but it happens. Humans are so visual if we can't see it, we don't think it's there.

When I look at the sky I get an aching in my heart to return to the sky. I somehow know I'm not of this Earth but I was born here and came here to learn. When I'm finished I'll be reunited with souls I've known for billions of years and we can see where we go from there.

No matter how we look at the possibility there maybe aliens out there watching us, some of it has to make sense. We want to go into outer space and explore, why? Don't we have everything we need here on Earth? Why would we want to go out into a dark place that has no heat, no air to breath or life as we know it? Does that really make sense to you? Or is our exploration of outer space just our way of feeling like we are headed home again?

Where did we get the idea that "god" or the "gods" came from the sky? Why didn't they come from the middle of the Earth? There are many stories of people living in middle Earth but not as many as from outer space or falling from the sky.

If we believe the story about Adam being created out of the dust of Earth, why wouldn't our god come from Earth too? Why would He/She be the only one that lives in the sky? That's just another point to ponder. And if you really read Genesis Chapter 1, Verse 26 it says, "And God said, "let US make man is OUR image, after OUR likeness, etc." Was God with someone? Who were "they", "us" and "our"? Was it us in soul form? What example did he use to get "our likeness"? How did he know what to make us look like?

Was there already someone here that looked like humans but were called Lemurians? Did "god" know the life force on Earth had to look at certain way? How would he know what humans were if there wasn't something that looked like them? How did he know what a man looked like or what a woman looked like? How many of "us" were there helping him decide what a human should look like? How did he know a fish needed water and a cat needed dry land? Where did this information come from?

Were there already gods on Earth that seemed to be solid or at least a form of our human-self? Is this why our physical bodies have the same elements as Earth, but our souls are pure energy? Even though souls are energy and there is energy on this planet, we don't seem to associate our souls with Earth at all. Our souls seem to be separate from the body in everyway.

The devil seems to come from middle Earth and seems to represent our dark side. So if the body is from Earth and the Devil lives under the Earth in Hell and God lives in outer space somewhere, then we have to be part of both of them. Our body has to be part of the devil or Earth and our soul is part of God. Did God ask the devil how to make humans in the image we are now so we could have a form that would be able to survive on Earth? And actually, the devil is never mentioned in Genesis. So who was the devil and did he "come from the sky as a fallen angel?" Or was he already here?

This got me thinking and wondering why the Bible didn't mention the devil at the beginning. I needed to know when the devil came into play because if we were all created at the same time, the devil should have been here with us. So I started researching "the story of the devil". I wondered if God was so great and made everything so good, why would he make a Devil and so much evil. Is the devil really a rogue alien or a fallen angel? In Job, the Bible says the devil helped inform God about what was happening on Earth. He wasn't evil at all in that story but a helpful entity to God.

I don't believe in the devil but because of all the stories about him, I figured there had to be something there. Maybe I just wasn't taking the devil seriously enough. Then I found it. The story of how the "fallen angel" came to be, at least the story I tend to believe. So here is a story about the devil that seems to persist even today that might explain "who" he is and where he came from and it's not from outer or even middle Earth.

John J. Robinson's "A Pilgrim's Path" explains that the word "Lucifer" was presented first in Isaiah 14:12 -

"How art thou fallen from heaven, O Lucifer, son of the morning! How art thou cut down to the ground, which didst weaken the nations!"

The first problem with this statement is that the name Lucifer is Latin, not Hebrew and it means Light and has nothing to do with darkness or evil. Also the original Hebrew text of Isaiah 14 was not about a fallen angel but about a fallen Babylonian king, who during his lifetime had persecuted the children of Israel. This whole devil story was about a king who had fallen from grace with the Jewish people because he had abuse so many of them.

In the original text there is no mention of Satan or a fallen angel, only a fallen king. So did someone want to create a great story to make a point? In Roman astronomy, the name Lucifer was given to the star we now know as the planet Venus. Lucifer meant morning star or light. It is thought that as scholars translated the Bible into English, they used varies versions of different languages and mistranslated the Hebraic metaphor of Lucifer. Through these many mistranslations, Lucifer is now known as Satan, the Devil and ironically the Prince of Darkness even through Lucifer means Light.

Behind every legion there is some amount of truth. The stories that have been past down from generation to generation maybe just stories but they had to come from somewhere just like the story about Satan, the truth was about a fallen king. So God still might be the only real alien who is looking down on us and we may still be our own worse devil.

It's funny how translations and meaning of words change over time. What means one thing today meant something else ten or even thousand years ago. Humans love to think and translate and try to understand the past, the present and the future. It's our biggest past time. We wonder what happened in the past and what will happen in the future. I wonder if all universes have "time and space" like we do?

Time is something that was created by man to help him feel balanced and in control of something. Time doesn't really exist. The sun rises, along with the morning star Lucifer, (just needed to throw that in there), and sets and would continue to do that without a clock or watch. We would still work and play without time, however we would probably do it when we felt like it instead of watching a clock. Think how a clock runs your life. We get up by one, we work by one, take coffee breaks by one, lunch, dinner, watch TV and the list goes on and on.

At the end of each "day" by what the clock says, we complain we ran out of "time". Or there wasn't enough time in the day to get everything done. Well, everyone gets the same amount of time. We either have from sun up to sun down or sun down to sun up. No one has anymore time than that. Some of us just manage our time better than others. However, if we didn't have time, we might just do what we wanted, when we wanted. That could be chaos because humans are not yet at the place of very good self-discipline.

When we're in spirit, there's no time at all. We just are! We're just doing what we're supposed to do. Do you think this is why souls or even aliens can time travel so quickly? After all, even in the Theory of Relativity, there is an "x" factor that makes anything possible. We're also on the cutting edge of learning quantum math but it can change everything we thought we knew.

I wonder if souls and aliens live by quantum math instead of our math. Do you think because souls and aliens have no concept of time it doesn't affect them? They just head out with a travel plan. They know it's going to take them awhile but because they have no time restrictions, they don't have to follow them. Their hyperdrive also doesn't adhere to the rules of time so they don't know what one billion light years are – it's just another Sunday drive in space to checkup on the Earthlings.

In many sci-fi shows, they portray the aliens as the bad guys. I believe this came from H.G. Well's story "The War of the Worlds" which put the nation into a panic. This fear of aliens coming to destroy us has persisted every since. This is really our human egos (which I like to call the real devil) getting in the way of ourselves and trying to make humans look better than the aliens. We look like the peaceful warriors in most of today's films. "We come in peace" but how can we come in peace when we can't even have peace on our own planet? Who's to say if aliens are bad or good? They might be like the legend of Satan – misunderstood or misinterpreted.

We should remember each universe is different and unique and there are many things out in space humans will never understand or even comprehend. Which brings us to space and what space is or isn't.

Here on Earth, nothing can be in the same space at the same time. In a three dimensional world, it's physically impossible. But what happens in outer space or in the spirit world? I know when we are in spirit form a thousand of us can fit into a very small space and be comfortable. We have the ability to make ourselves as big or little as we want – here is where the shape-shifting comes in too. I feel we're naturals at it but have just forgotten how to do it.

However the question still remains, what is space and how do we let it affect us in this world compared to other universes? Do other aliens find they have to adhere to the rules of space or is space just a spot that can be changed, filled in or moved to accommodate whatever they want to do with it? And do they really understand space better than we do?

Space is around us all the time. We stand in space, we live in space, we walk in space and we move through space all day long. Our body goes through several different energy fields everywhere we go. These energy fields have different affects on us that we may not be conscious of. It's really fun to walk consciously into a room and feel the different energies it has. Each energy takes up space too. The question is "can an energy form and a solid form occupy the same space?" I'm not sure any of us can answer that for sure.

We know no one can occupy the same space we are in, not in this dimension and if we really look at it, we occupy the same space all the time. That space is wherever we are at any given time. The only space we really own is our aura which never goes away and always goes with us. We move through space but our personal space is what is around us not where we're standing or sitting.

We have no claim to any space that is outside our aura system because that's the beginning of outer space and everyone has the right to explore it. The outer space where the stars are is the same principle. Anyone can explore it and move through it but they can't occupy it. It's just not possible.

So what do aliens know about space and space travel that we don't? If they have a super space ship that moves at light speed or faster, that means they have mastered time as well as space. So you see; Star Trek isn't as far out there as you might think. We could be doing this in another 3 to 4 thousand years – then we will really be the aliens.

Here on planet Earth, we've just begun to explore the possibilities of matter and anti-matter as a power source but what if other civilizations mastered this a million years ago. Could this be why they don't have to play by our rules? We think we know it all but we're just babies learning to walk. We still have at least 4.5 billion years here and just think what we can do between now and then.

Another question I like to ask is, "why are we so interested in outer space and yet we don't even know our own Earth that well?"

We haven't explored the seas to their fullest or even the forests and mountains. As I stated earlier, no one really thought the city of Troy was real until they uncovered it. So why do we think Atlantis is still a myth? Shouldn't we get to know our own planet better before we go off into outer space? Maybe if we took more time to study Earth and it's secrets, we might find out more about ourselves. After all, everything we've ever needed has always been here. Nothing I know of has ever dropped from the sky to supply us with something we need.

Of course there have been rocks from meters and comets but they haven't helped us make bricks, cement or plastic. It might have given us more knowledge to understand the elements of the universe and what we are made of but they have raised more questions, not answered them.

So look to the sky at night and see what you feel. Look to it during the day and see if you can't see a quick twinkle of a star, even with the sun shining. Think about the planets in our solar system and all the ones being formed billions of light years away from us in outer space.

Then remember where you are and the limits you have on your body. Try to find out the answers about your inner space before you go into outer space. Once you find the inner space answers and understand yourself, you can then move to the outer space dimension – whether it's just across the street or going to the moon.

Look at the people around you and know that all of us are aliens in some way or another. None of us are really of this Earth, just our bodies. When we step out of them, we are truly in our natural form.

Ghosts – What's real and what's not

If our soul leaves our body when we die and goes home or back into the spirit world, what are ghosts?

There are several different kinds of "ghosts" or energies that hang around after the body has died.

Sometimes when a person dies, they don't want to go into the Light and go home. This is another point of how much free will we have. Some people want to stay on Earth for a lot of different reasons.

They are still attached to their home and want to live there longer

They died very quickly and refuse to acknowledge they are really dead.

They think the loved ones they left behind still need them.

They really want to haunt a person, place or thing

So let's look into some of these phenomenon and see if we can make some sense out of them.

When a person lives in the same place for a long time, be it a house, prison or cave, they are imprinting their energy in that place. I just did a reading for a lady the other day and she asked about her mother-in-law who had crossed several months earlier.

I sat there for a moment waiting for the energy of the deceased woman to come into the room and when it did, I was amazed. I saw a picture of a house in my mind and this was what I heard, "I'm still in the house and I'm not leaving. I lived there for 30 years and no one is going to tell me where I need to go."

I told my client what I had heard and she didn't seem surprised at all. "She was a mean, stubborn woman in life so I guess she's that way over there too. Is she going to haunt the place?" My client asked.

The answer rang in my ear "YES!"

The mother-in-law had no want to leave the house and was going to make sure everyone who entered knew she was there. This is a case of being attached to Earthly things and not wanting to give them up. We all know we can't take our possessions with us but I bet not many of you thought about just staying here with them.

I don't know if the mother-in-law will really haunt the house but she isn't going any where else soon. Besides, if we live forever, haunting a place for the next 100 to 1000 years is nothing. Remember when we are in spirit, there is no time or space.

When there is a spirit that is actually haunting a place, it's known as an intelligent haunting. That means the spirit is really here and not just implanted energy. The soul has made a conscious choice to stay on Earth. Some people think they're stuck if they don't go into the Light and leave this plane of existence, but no soul is really ever stuck. There are always guides and angels watching over all of us waiting to help us.

I've run into some spirits that seem to be "stuck" in a place that's not Earth but not in the Light or dark either. Many times these are souls who are looking for someone that didn't die with them. They might be children who are looking for their parents, however the angels do their best to guide all souls into the Light. If a soul wants to stay in a gray area, that's their choice. This is another example of how much "free will" we have.

There have been a few times when I've run into a spirit that isn't sure they are dead or are afraid to go into the Light. Usually with a little talking too, they turn and walk into the Light and find what they're looking for. It's much simpler than what you see in the movies. Movies are made to scare us but it's not the real world of spirit and ghosts so don't get too caught up in it.

I have found most of the time you can talk to spirits and get them to move on or out or into the Light; as long as they aren't dark entities. If they are dark entities, you might need assistance. When a spirit moves into the Light, angels, family members, spirit guides and other souls are there to meet them and help them cross.

That also brings up a point about our loved ones visiting us. They have the free will to check in on us whenever they want too. However, checking in and interfering with our lives are two very different things. Checking in means they're visiting and making sure we are okay. They can even give us suggestions about the choices we might want to make to help us along our path. Many of us have relatives and friends that come around to help us all the time and we don't even know it. We usually know when they're near by a feeling we get in our body or a thought about them. Because they're in spirit, they can send us thought patterns and we start thinking about them. Spirits don't have vocal cords, because they don't have a body, so they have to communicate thru telepathy.

When you get a thought about a person who has crossed, thank them and talk to them. They can hear you. You can tell them anything you want and ask them for help in making choices or decisions. They can give you signs but the final choice is always up to you.

You know the Bible says, "Ask and it shall be given". Well most of us forget to ask. We think we are asking too much or someone will get mad at us for asking. Nothing could be farther from the truth. We have to ask in order for our helpers to have the permission to help us. It's against spiritual law for anyone to tell us what to do, even our angels. They can offer guidance and suggestions but the final choice is always ours.

It's just like here on Earth. When someone helps us without our asking them for help, we either get mad, it turns out badly or they feel used. When we ask someone to help us, we are telling them we are unable or unsure of something and need help. We are actually opening an energy doorway so another person can help us. We are asking for suggestions or ways to do things that might be easier for us. This is a big difference from being told what to do. Remember guides and angels are helpers for you, most of the time ghosts are just hanging around where they feel the most comfortable. There are exceptions to everything but for the most part a ghost will not give you guidance.

Asking is part of getting to know your spirit guides and angels. Asking and talking to them helps you feel their energy and distinguish between them, a dark entity and a ghost.

Here are some of the things I ask my guides and angels for. I ask for parking places, for pennies on the ground as a sign they are with me, I ask for protection wherever I go and for so much more. The more you ask for the little things, the better you get at asking for the big things. However, be careful what you ask for. I always ask for something and then say, "Let it come to me in the best way for my soul and all the souls involved."

The Universe will bring it to you when the time is right and how it's supposed to come to you. Don't judge it, just let it be. Because the energy of "asking" has a vibration of its own, the like vibration will come back to you in the way it's supposed too, not the way you might want it to come to you.

But what about the souls who are hanging around Earth? The ones we might see or feel around us. We need to become more conscious of their energy verses our spirit guides energy and that just takes practice. Also, don't judge a soul that wants to stay around this dimension for awhile but don't feel sorry for them either. It's their free will. Many times they have a lot of fun just hanging around and watching everything that's happening here on Earth.

However, there are times when a soul dies so quickly, they don't think their dead. This quick death can confuse a soul. This is when we need to talk to them and tell them it's okay to go into the Light and greet the other people there.

I've run into ghosts who all of a sudden look at me like I'm the ghost! And who's to say I'm not. We see each other when the conditions are right and I look as much like a ghost to them as they do to me. Many times they disappear right away because of the shock of seeing each other.

This kind of "seeing each other" can also be an intelligent haunting. They can knock on things because they hear us knock on things. Most of the time there is a time delayed reaction when we ask them to do something because of the energy transfer involved from one dimension to another but that's just the way energy works.

Let's look at what happens between the third and fourth dimension when we are trying to communicate with a soul. First, when they hear us, the sound is slow and seems heavy and drawn out. This is because the energy here is heavier. Our voices sound low and so slow they have trouble understanding what we're saying.

When we hear souls from the other side, the sound is faster and sometimes even sounds like buzzing or ringing in our ears. This is because their vibration is so much higher than ours and our ears can not detect some of what they are saying. However, our dogs and cats usually do hear them and that's why our pets run from it or bark at empty air.

Because a crossed soul's vibration is back to a pure energy form, it's very hard to hear them. They might be talking in full sentences but we might only hear a word or two. This is why we "think" we hear someone but aren't sure. Plus their sounds will be at a different pitch than our sounds – hence dogs and cats hear them. In saying this, they don't have vocal cords like we do but because sound is energy and vibration, they can make noises and form the vibration of words.

I know that seems strange to some of you but sound is only a vibration and each sound has its own unique vibration. It's like the strings on a guitar. Each one has a different sound. Souls on the other side are very good at controlling energy and making it work for them so they can form words with energy. That's why a recording of a ghosts' voice sounds so strange to us and is hard to understand. Not only is it in a different dimension, the energy is somewhat different as it travels through that dimension.

Sometimes they have to flicker lights or knock on things to make us realize they're near. They can't always materialize in front of us or make words. It takes too much energy.

We've heard for a long time that ghosts will pull on the energy in a room to help them materialize in this dimension. I'm not sure it's to materialize as much as it helps them to lower their vibration so they can join us in this dimension. I think they have enough energy to do what they want, but they need to match a lower vibration to become visible. If they want you to see them in a certain room or place, they have to match some of the energy vibration in that place. I feel they pull on the Earth's heavy energy to help them match the vibration of Earth therefore making themselves visible to us. To see something in this dimension it has to match or have some qualities of this dimension.

Each dimension has it's own vibration and so we can't see things in these dimensions most of the time. That doesn't mean they aren't there or don't exist. That would be like saying the stars aren't shining during the day. Of course none of us knows how it works but I know it works. I can see things in another dimension if I just look and be in the present moment. If I watch what my vibration and energy level is like, I can experience new and different things in another dimension.

Let me see if I can explain this. When you've eaten a big, heavy dinner, you feel full and slow. Your bodies' vibration has been slowed down because of the extra weight of the food it's trying to digest. Remember every action has a reaction to it and every action and reaction have a different vibration to them too. When you aren't full of food, your body can vibrate at a higher level because there is one less activity or action it has to do. The more activity your body is doing in different directions, the less it can vibrate in one direction. When you are focused on one thing or activity, you are naturally focusing your vibration on that one thing. Even if we are just sitting back after a big meal and watching TV, it gives our body the change to focus on digesting food without having to do much of anything else.

If I want to see something in the 4th dimension, I focus on that dimension and try to get my body's energy vibration to match it. Just like a ghost focuses their energy on our dimension so they can lower their vibration to match ours so we can see them. Sometimes we don't even realize this is happening. Sometimes, like when we are meditating, just focusing on what we want will get us connected to it and things just happen. It's a matter of raising or lowering your own personal vibrational space to match another vibrational space. That's the magic of the universe.

So we can manually raise or lower our vibrations by our thoughts. If we are thinking about doing something that has a dark energy around it, say like killing someone, our vibration will lower to that dark energy vibration. If we are thinking about loving someone, our vibration will raise. There have been all kinds of experiments done to prove that a thought of love vibrates at a different level than the thought of hate. So it's really the vibration behind your thoughts that can create or not create what you want.

Many of us have had the following experience. When we're just about to fall asleep, we think we hear or see something. We're experiencing something from a different dimension because our vibration at the time is different than when we're fully awake. We're relaxed and allowing our energy to go to a different place. When we do this, we're entering another world. It's a great place to visit but because we have a body and have to keep a lower vibration to stay in the body, we can't live there. We have to live in this dimension with this body. When we leave the body, we can do anything we want, almost. We can't come back to Earth and stay here in this dimension unless we lower our vibration which means entering a human body.

So ghosts can come and visit us but can't stay in this dimension for a long time unless they jump into a body of some kind and that can happen.

Before we get into how souls can jump into our bodies, let's first explore the good and the not so good souls. Many people think if you are bad or mean on this side, you're that way on the other side; that's not necessary true. We all have to learn to be nice, mean, loving, hateful and many other things so we can learn what life on this planet is all about.

Many souls are very loving when they cross to the other side even if they were mean here. I believe all souls have some love in them but many times we have to look deep and dig even deeper to find it. Some souls have been in the dark for thousands of years and it's hard for them to get out. It's just like our bad habits here on Earth. We know we don't have to do them, but it's difficult to change our patterns.

Many souls have decided to stay in a dark place and that's their free will. These are spirits we need to stay away from however let's clear up some misunderstandings about dark beings. There are dark beings who have been human and dark beings who haven't been human. The dark beings that have been human can be ghosts and spirits we see, hear, smell or feel in some other way. The dark beings that haven't been human are the demons we hear about that take a different form most of the time. They usually just want to scare us so they take form as a dark cloud or a monster of some kind.

Remember when Jesus cast out the seven demons into the swine? Well these energies, which were really our human emotions and egos, had already been around for thousand of years and are still with us today. Demons are energies that throughout time have evolved into entities because we have given them more and more energy and power. Remember, we can create anything we want. The energy we supply them with is greed, guilt, jealousy, anger and anything that has to do with taking control. And the one last thing we do is believe in them, which makes them real.

These demons are energy and haven't been human so they don't fully understand their impact on humanity. These demons understand they are making humans miserable and scared but they think it's funny. They like to see how they can make us react to their haunting or cruel actions. We have literally created a monster out of thin air.

Many times these beings will impress their dark energies on us and make us feel uneasy. This feeling taps into our dark emotions and makes them start flooding to the surface. Have you ever felt a sudden rush of jealousy or anger and wondered where it came from? Many times this energy is from a dark being. They can put their energy on us and make us feel like something is wrong even when it's not. It's the opposite energy of an angel. When angels are around us, we feel safe and peaceful. Demons just bring out the worst in us like angels bring out the best.

Demons will enlist the help of souls who have not gone into the Light. Because demons haven't lived in the human body, for any length of time, they have to call on others who know what humans feel. You see, a demon can come into a body but they can't stay forever because of the vibration. The body will even start to die when a demon is in it too long. Their vibration is slower than the bodies and it can't seem to match a human vibration. It's very hard on a body.

Demons call on and use souls who have decided to stay in the darkness for one reason or another. Some of these souls were mass murders on this side or wizards that think the darkness gives them more power than the Light. These dark souls know how to keep their vibrational rate at the human rate longer than a demon because they were once human. They are great tools for the demons to use because they do what the demon tells them to do. Also, demons will recognize a dark soul if its born into a human body. The dark energy is something demons recognize right away and will follow these humans around. They will communicate with them and have these humans do their nasty deeds in this dimension.

These dark humans are very easy to control because they have the same dark vibration as many demons. The demons just attach themselves and away they go on the humans' shoulder whispering nasty things in their ears. They can get dark humans to do anything at anytime because the humans have turned their free will over to the demons. It's the same principal as if we just do what everyone else wants us to do with our lives but we don't do what we want. We are really giving our free will away.

Demons have been around for a very long time and as long as we give Demons power by believing in them, they will always be around. Many demons are energies we've created by believing in and living on the dark side for too long. Because everything is really just energy, these energies have gained power and manifested into their own forces over thousands and thousands of years of putting energy into them. It's like us thinking about inventing something or making something in our lives. If we believe in it enough, it starts to happen. Same with many demon forces.

Just like the implanted energy we talked about earlier where people have lived for a long time, if you believe in something long enough, you can manifest it. We're here to create and there is nothing we can't create; good or evil.

Remember you can call on the devil, which is the dark side or you can ask an angel.

It's said by many that we create our own diseases, belief systems, fears, needs and everything else we live through each day. If we can create that, we can certainly create demons to haunt us. If you look at the Middle East, it's now a barren wasteland in many regions where there used to be green lush fields. Years of hate, war and dark energy has been implanted in the Earth's crust there and turned it into a dry, cracked hard land. Could this hard, dry crusty layer really be a protective layer so the negative energy can't go all the way down to the Earth's core?

If you really look at how Mother Earth protects herself from us humans, you would see that no matter what we do, she'll take care of herself. It's really quite awesome. If everyone in all the warring countries stopped hating and killing each other, the land would heal and the Earth would return to its natural balance. But alas, we humans aren't there yet. We still live in fear of the "everything" and the "nothing".

I believe if everyone stopped believing in demons, the energy would start to lessen and within a few hundred years there would be no more demons. This could help many dark souls go into the Light because they wouldn't be supplied with the energy of our fears which is really their food. Once the "feeding of the fear" had ended in humans, they would have little or no power in the dark and would have no real purpose to be there.

If we really think about it, we are our own worse demon. We put dark energy into the world every day. When we think any negative thought about someone else, the governments around the world, the way our neighbor acts or thinks, we are just adding to the dark side and giving demons more power.

It'll take several thousand years to get people to understand and to stop being afraid of life. It'll take generations to become aware of what we can do or become if we really put our mind to it. It'll take thousands or even millions of years because we really have to do it one person at a time. The reason it will take time is because so many people don't want to change. They don't like it and they don't want any part of it, which is a shame because change equals growth. Humans also want proof a change is going to be better before they do it. There's no guarantee about that either. The good news is you can be one of the first people and show others how it can be done. All you have to do is stop your negative thinking.

I like to embrace the bad news on TV with thoughts like this.

"You can't heal anything unless it's brought out into the Light – so let the healing begin"

"Bless them and give them grace and I pray they see they are hurting others"

"I pray we learn by our choices"

This kind of thinking keeps the devil and your demons from the front door. Remember a demon can't hurt you unless you give them the energy or power to hurt you. I know there are some of you out there that say, "Oh no, I had a demon that wouldn't leave me alone no matter what I did."

Well, somewhere deep inside you had to believe in that demon and that's enough to give it the energy to bother you. It's like a curse – a curse can't harm you unless you believe in it, then your sub-conscious takes over and will feed energy into the curse and make it happen.

If you have one little doubt somewhere in your body or mind, a dark being will pick it out no matter how small it is. Remember we talked earlier about how our thoughts put out cords of energy and starts to look for the energy that matches it. This works with curses and dark energy too. Doubt is something we should try to get over.

I laugh at a curse just as I laugh at a demon. When I do a house clearing, I demand the ghost or demon appear in front of me. I show no fear, none. I've only had one ghost show me some blue smoke and I laughed at his attempt to show himself. I then smudged and sprinkled holy water around the house to change the vibration. Because the smudging and the sprinkling of holy water are done in love, there is a vibrational shift.

A dark entity doesn't like the higher "love" vibration and will usually leave. However doing this kind of clearing can also give a dark entity the change to raise their vibration to match it. Once they have raised their vibration with love, more Light vibration as entered their space and they begin to change. This is when you can tell them if they stay they have to go into the Light because their vibration has been raised. Most will move on and be very thankful you helped them into the Light.

Even some ghost hunters and psychics put out a fear when they are looking for spirits on the other side and this will bring many dark beings to them. Any fear at all is energy and these dark energies will grab it and eat it up. I know it's hard not to fear the unseen and unknown because we have been taught for thousands of years to fear everything we can't see or don't understand. We have to be the new generation that is stopping this fearful way of life. We have to start understanding we are creating our own worse nightmares by fearing these things.

Back in the days of the Lemurians, there seemed to be no demons. The Lemurians came and went and shape shifted into things. They were all about love and learning and feared nothing because they knew there was nothing to fear. They could do anything and be anything. It was fun exploring all the new creations. It was fun taking form in this universe.

I think fear only came after the human body started to form. This fear was the fear of being stuck here. When that happened, all the other fears started to come into play. The fear of not having enough food, water, land to live on and finally after thousands of years of sharing and bartering, we created money and even turned it into a fear of never having enough.

If we stopped putting so much power and energy into money, it would go away and we could put our time and energy into learning and enjoying this place we call Earth. But I think we are stuck in this "money thing" for awhile because the human conscious changes slowing. The more people you have in a group, the slower the process of getting any one thing done. This is because we all have our own ideas and free will. But I regress — we were talking about demons. Let's talk about how a demon can get into the human body.

When we drink alcohol or do drugs, we are creating a hole in our aura and energy field for any spirit to enter. Spirits in the Light will not enter your body unless they are invited. Psychics channel Light Beings all the time when they are doing readings. I'm channeling information as

I'm writing this book. I invite in whoever is in the Light and would like to help me. However a dark soul will take any opportunity to come into a human body to have some fun and then it leaves in a way that usually makes the body feel bad in some way. An example of this can be a headache, upset stomach, we feel "off" or there can be anger and frustration.

When someone is drunk or on drugs, we have all heard the saying, "He's not himself". Well, there's more truth in that saying than we may realize. When someone is not in his "right mind" or "in his body", the body is left vulnerable to any spirit to come into it.

You see, when we are abusing our body this way, many times our soul can't stay in the body because we are screwing up the vibration of the body. However, dark souls don't mind the abusively low energy of drugs and alcohol because their vibration is at a lower rate already. This is because they are still very close to the Earth and vibrational pull of Earth. Souls who have entered the Light when they died have a lighter vibration and aren't as attached to Earth. So dark souls just jump right into a body at certain times. (When I'm taking about vibrations, it's like colors we see. Every color vibrates at a different vibration to make that color. The more light you bring into a color, the higher the vibration.)

When we are not present in our bodies, there is always a chance of another soul coming into it. It's like an empty shell without our spirit in it and is open to any energy. We need to stay in it and in the present moment to really protect it against unwelcomed visitors.

When someone isn't acting like "themselves" as we call it, you can bet another entity, has come into them.

It's like when someone is channeling a Light spirit from the other side. A person who channels spirits has to put up protection before they start channeling or they might be asking for a dark soul to come in and spread lies. This is why you need to be careful about who you listen too.

Not all people who channel are channeling Light beings. A dark soul can come in and be deceitful and tell lies. This is very important to remember. So how do you know the difference? Easy – a Light soul will always have a positive outlook on events no matter what they are. A dark soul will try to spread fear and mistrust because that's the energy they need more of to survive in their dark place.

If we drink or do drugs a lot, a dark soul can start to take over our bodies. Because their vibration is already lower than Light beings, they can match our Earth vibration at a much faster and easier pace. They don't have to work so hard at it and if we are letting them enter us every night or even three times a week, they are stealing away some of our vibration and energy each time. This gives them a better opportunity to stay in our body longer and longer each time. They can eventually take over completely. They zap some of our energy every time they enter and leave our body so we feel tired or upset. We might even find it hard to stay in our body and that's when we leave an opening for a dark soul to enter.

Why would a dark soul want to come into our bodies in the first place? Well, this way they don't have to be born again. It saves them the trauma of birth and having to start over. They just jump into a body. They remember what they were going before they died and they continue from where they left off. It's an easy way to come back to Earth but it's not the right way.

If we all did this, we would remember a lot more about our past lives but then we wouldn't learn anything new either. I believe we have to go through the trauma of birth and death to learn and grow and experience what life is in several different ways. It's all about coming back rich, poor, tall, short, thin, and fat or whatever way we have contracted to come back so we can experience things. Each birth is different, besides we have to bond with our parents and other family members because they are in our lives for a reason.

Dark souls take over bodies just so they can continue from where they left off before they died. They are doing the same dark deeds and making themselves and others miserable. They haven't completed the process of living, dying, having a life review to see what they learned and what they didn't. I don't believe we can learn anything by doing this. So they are really stuck on the same path because they have to finish their lessons and they haven't.

If they would have gone into the Light they would have seen where they might have done things better or the lessons they learned. They could have started fresh in another body but that's the hard way of doing things and dark souls always look for the easy way out. Dark souls have as much free will as anyone else so they can walk into us at any time, if we let them.

No two souls can occupy the same body space at the same time. They can come and go in a nano-second but not in the same exact space. However, body space is negotiable. Because our souls are energy and can be as big as we want or as small as we want, you can have two souls in the same body in different locations. You could be in your body and someone else in your head or visa versa.

So don't abuse your body and don't invite other beings in. Light beings can always talk to you or be with you without being in you. Dark beings can do the same and usually start out that way. Then when they have their grip of fear around our hearts and sub-conscious, they move in. This may sound strange but anything is possible when you are talking about energy. So watch what you do to your body and who you might be inviting in when you least expect it.

Remember your sub-conscious runs your body and if you put it and your conscious self to sleep with drugs or alcohol, anyone can enter. This can lead to what we call demonic possession of the body. This is a haunting and can lead to all kinds of trouble.

Demonic possessions are very rare! To help the person get rid of the take-over, you really need professional help and you need to have the person WANT to get rid of the demon. Many people don't want to get rid of the demon. They are afraid to let go and live their life. The demon actually gives them an excuse to act badly or be a victim and get the attention they want. It's sad but true.

Ghosts, souls who have lived as humans on Earth and died, and demons, energies who haven't been human but have had enough negative energy pumped into them to come to life, live in a different dimension then humans. Because of this dimensional difference, their energy vibration is different.

We can make demons stay where they're at by not giving them any more power or energy by fearing them. It's only when we give them power they can pull on it and meet us for a short while in our dimension. So it's important not to give them any power or feel fear. Demons don't have the power we think they do unless we give it to them. They have never been human and it's harder for them to match our vibration. People who practice devil worship have to "conjure" up the devil or call to him and that gives the dark side power.

Many ghosts, because they have been human before, can match the human vibration easier and be seen or make their presence known. I have found it easier to get in touch with souls on the other side of veil since my near death out of body experience. I believe it's because I was in the vibration of the spirit world and then came back into my body. My soul can recognize the vibration of souls who have crossed easier because of what I have experienced and remembered. There are thousand of people who have had out of body experiences that don't do what I do and some don't even remember their experience. I'm just one of the lucky ones, I guess.

Another type of haunting is implanted energy haunting. This is where the implanted energy of a person or animal is played back again and again without the soul being present. This happens all the time to me when I'm driving on a highway where a deer or other animal has been killed. I'll see the animal along the side of the road for just a brief second and think it's really standing there – but then it's gone. Most of the time this kind of haunting is silent and looks the same all the time.

This will happen many times when a person or animal is killed very suddenly. The imprint of their energy stays in the area. It plays over and over again just like a video without any interaction. This is only energy caught in time and we really don't understand it or why it happens but it does. We don't know everything about energy yet and how it works, but it's the main force for everything on this planet. Energy will fade out if there is no more energy put into something.

An example of how energy fades is love. If we love someone, we are putting out an energy to connect with them. This love energy is renewed everyday by our thoughts of love for them. When we stop loving them, we stop thinking about them so much. We don't connect with them and soon their memory fades from us.

This can happen in a haunting too. If we go to a place and know it's haunted and want to see the ghosts or something happen, we are putting energy into it. We are giving energy to something to keep it alive. If no one goes to this place for a thousand years, there probably won't be a haunting because the energy has faded.

Energy is like a camp fire. You have to keep putting wood on it to keep it burning. Stop the wood and it will eventually die out. Some of the wood will burn out in a couple of hours. Some will take days to cool completely and the ground can stay warm for weeks. It depends on the type of wood that was burning, how much was burning and how long it was burning. Look at energy in the same way.

We should understand that not every "bump in the night" is a haunting or a spirit from the other side. Many times it's just energy moving around. It could be the house settling, the wind blowing or any number of other things. Energy can move and make noise just like the wind, after all there isn't much difference between the two of them. They are both unseen but can create sound or make things move. With billions of people sending out thoughts of energy there's bound to be a lot of unseen energy moving around in our atmosphere at all times. Our energy bodies will pick up on some of this energy too and if the energy gets to be too much, sound or events can happen that we can't explain; but that doesn't mean it's a ghost or spirit.

I've put some questions down to ask yourself when you think there might be a paranormal event going on.

If you think you feel, see or hear a disembodied spirit of a human or animal ask yourself, did they know they were going to cross just before it happened? How did they cross? Was it fast or slow? How long had they lived or walked the land where they crossed? What is the energy of land or building like? Is there a vortex or other energy window in this location? Does the event only happen on the day they were killed? Does the event happen routinely or just ever now and then? Is there noise or knocking with the event or is it silent?

Could what you are hearing be mice in the walls or floor? Could the house just be settling? Could you have a build up of energy in your house or on the land? Could someone be playing tricks on you? Are you hearing voices that are on the astro-plane or in the universal energy port and they have nothing to do with you?

All these questions should be asked and answered before you can move forward with what kind of paranormal event might be taking place. Just because there's vision or sound doesn't mean it's someone trying to get in touch with you.

One of the biggest mistakes people make is thinking every "bump in the night" is a person from the other side trying to contact us. It's so much easier for these souls to meet us in our dreams. When we are dreaming, we are usually out of our bodies and our vibration is raised. Thus we can meet other souls on the astro-plane where their vibration is normal. We can even meet another "live" human on the astro-plane in our dreams.

Here is an example of this. Years ago one of my girlfriends came to me very excited about a dream she had. She told me she had a spiritual question and needed an answer. Her guides told her to call me. In her dream, she picked up the phone and dialed my number. She remembered me answering the phone but not what I said to her.

I smiled and said, "That's funny because I dreamt you called me and I picked up the phone."

I know she and I had communicated on the astro-plane that night and whatever information she had been looking for was passed on through our souls connecting. It wasn't important that our conscious minds understood it; our souls got it.

Meeting someone or a pet on the astro-plane is so much easier on everyone. The problem with this is we don't usually remember our dreams. When we wake up and open our eyes, our brain starts checking the status of our body. This is what our brain does as we wake up.

"Okay, eyes are starting to open, yes we have a go on the eyes. The heart is still pumping, the lungs are working fine. I can feel my fingers, toes and other extremities. Oh boy, the bladder is working overtime. Need to get up and empty it."

Meanwhile, the part of your brain that was trying to hang on to the dream you just had is already taking you to the bathroom. The dream goes down the toilet, so to speak.

If you can not think about anything but your dream when you first wake, you have a better chance of remembering it. Don't think about your feet, hands, heart or bladder – just think about what you were dreaming about. That should help. We all travel out of our bodies at night. The soul needs no sleep. This is part of living forever.

Many times this travel is a way of meeting our ghosts and demons. Many times these energies are just our own fears and we have to meet them when we are in spirit to get a handle on them. Dreams can inform us and help us in many ways. Dreams are also a great release for our sub-conscious and problems that are bothering us. We can meet our spirit guides and talk to them about what to do next in our life. Dreams in many cases are extensions of our human life.

We don't always understand them but they are a fact of life; one of the many mysteries we may never understand as long as we are in human form. Another part of this mystery are the ghosts and demons that are as much a part of this universe as the spirit guides and angels and the longer we give them energy and power, the longer they will be here.

Suicide

Let's talk about this event for a few moments. Our society has been taught suicide is one of the worst things a person can do, but is it really?

In the animal kingdom when an animal is sick, old or weak, they go away from the rest of the herd, flock or even their partner because they know two things are happening.

1. They are sending out pheromones that tell predator they are old, weak or sick. These pheromones will bring the predators close to them so they go off by themselves thus protecting the rest of the herd from the predators.

2. They know they are dying and many times they welcome predators to end their life fast to stop the suffering. Some even go looking for predators to commit a kind of suicide.

Could this act of wanting to die quickly be hiding in our genes from thousands of years ago? We are part of the animal kingdom so there has to be a connection to all of this.

Now I'm not saying suicide is right or wrong but we shouldn't judge a person for it.

Here's what I've learned when I do readings on souls who have committed suicide. They usually have remorse at committing this act after they see how they have hurt the ones they left behind. They usually don't feel remorse in doing the act, but it's the affect on others they regret.

Many psychics have said they find these souls come back right away, I haven't run into this. People who commit suicide do need to come back to finish their lessons but remember "free will" is what this life is all about. If they need to rest and regroup, then they can rest and regroup. What good would a soul be in another life if they came back right away and still had the idea of suicide on their minds?

I also don't like to call these souls "victims of suicide". There are no victims unless we let ourselves be a victim. Thinking you're a victim makes you a victim. If we look at everything in our lives as a lesson or something that made you stronger, you can't be a victim.

I've been through a lot in my life; from sexual child abuse to an abuse marriage and cancer, but I wouldn't change a thing. I'm not a victim and I am able to help people who are going through what I went through. I've been there and know what they are talking about and how they feel.

If death is only an illusion to experience, then maybe we are supposed to experience suicide in at least one life time to see what it's like. We won't know for sure until we cross. I do know if we end our life before we're finished with our lessons, we have to come back at some point and finish but I believe we can pick when we want to come back.

I don't want anyone to think I'm saying suicide is okay. I'm just saying we judge it and the soul who commits the act too harshly. We shouldn't judge it at all. Usually someone who commits suicide has problems they can't handle anymore. If we judge them, we are putting more negative energy on a soul who is trying to get away from their own negative energy. We should be giving them grace and love.

I've seen people commit suicide from physical, mental or emotional pain and even just laziness about living. I don't judge anyone because I didn't know what their full contract is all about. I've worked with people who want to commit suicide and this is what I tell them.

"No one can really stop you if you want to do this. You'll find a way if you really want too die. What I ask of you is not to take anyone with you! Don't shoot the person you're mad at and then yourself. Just kill yourself and let others be.

When you're body's dead, your soul won't go to hell. I don't believe in hell. You do have the choice of going into the Light or staying in a dark place. If you stay in the dark place of depression, you really are in a hell and this can happen. It happens because you were depressed when you killed yourself and you haven't gotten over it. So think about it very carefully first.

If you do go into the Light, you get to have a life review. This review will reveal what you were supposed to do here on Earth. If you ended your life early and didn't complete everything, you'll have to come back and start over again.

What lessons or purpose you didn't complete can be as small as meeting a stranger on the street and smiling at them or as big as not having a child you were supposed to bring into this world. You'll never know until you get to the other side.

Now do you want to risk having to come back and relive everything you have lived up to this point just so you finish what you came here to do? Or would you rather try living one day at a time and see what happens? You know, you might die tomorrow of a heart attack or in an accident and it's the way you are really supposed to die. You could die tomorrow because your contract is fulfilled and then you won't have to come back.

I'd think about it and see if what you're going through is just a lesson and will end soon or if you want to end it too soon. If you let the lesson end on its own, you can get on with a wonderful life. If you end the lesson too soon, you have to come back and experience it again to finish it.

Now the choice is still up to you, but think about it for a few days and see how you feel then."

That's how I feel about suicide. Most of the people on the other side who take their own life are sorry when they see their life review. They see what they were going through. They see if they would have hung in there, things would have gotten better. If they would have waited for awhile, they wouldn't have ended their life.

There is always an exception to this and some people are just ready to go home. They aren't sorry. They knew what they were doing and they were ready to go home and rest and that's okay. Being human is a hard thing to be and not all souls can handle it; however life is a precious event for a soul. Angels call us their "heroes" because we have chosen to come to Earth and be human. It's a hard thing to do but any alien or solid life form is harder than being just pure energy.

I've heard that angels have never been human and can't really understand everything we go through but they are there to help us in anyway they can. If we decide to jump off a 40 foot high building to end our life, they won't stop us. On the way down they'll whisper in our ear, "Not a wise choice" but they won't judge us or leave our side. In fact, they might even help us jump out of our bodies before we hit the ground. That would save us a lot of pain.

Life is something we take for granted most of the time. I think that's because some where deep inside we know we can't die. The body will die but not the soul. But even with saying that, life as a human is a great gift and should be looked at as an honor. When we die, we take back a lot of knowledge for other souls.

All souls bring back knowledge with them to help other souls before they reincarnate. Remember life is a joint effort on everyone's part to learn, grow and experience. I don't think we understand this concept to its fullest. It never stops. It's like the energizer bunny – it just keeps going and going and going.

I feel even our creator doesn't know where it will lead because our "free will" changes things all the time. I think it makes it interesting for him too. He has built in all the choices we might make but to watch each of us go in a different direction to get to the same end has to be entertaining! It's like watching ants.

If we make conscious choices about our lives, take the responsibility for those choices, don't expect anything from anyone else, work together for the good of everyone and find something good in everything, it might be a better world.

We can learn from our "free will" choices not to be a victim or we can get lost in being a victim. Free will can tell you not to let the selfish choice of someone else affect you in a negative way. That's what free will is really all about.

If we stopped and thought for a moment before we did anything and remembered there is some kind of action or reaction for every other action, reaction, or thought, we wouldn't do half the dumb stuff we do.

Think about what I just said. If we knew we were going to get back what we put out, wouldn't we think more about what we do and say? If we knew we would get back something negative when we did something negative, we wouldn't do it. Our common sense would tell us not to. But alas, not many of us have any common sense left. It walked out the door holding hands with responsibility.

You can learn lessons from watching others but never condemn them. We'll never know what another soul needs to experience to make their contract complete. Suicide is something we don't understand and that's okay.

I tell people if they don't "get" something this lifetime, they're not supposed to "get" it. It's that's simple. Make life simple and you can't go wrong.

Well enough about this subject. We know we live forever and we have the free will to do what we want. Each of us has their own path to walk.

So let's go on to something a little more fun and see if we can make sense out of age, beauty and all that body stuff.

Age, Beauty and All that Body Stuff

I think I'm at an age where I can write about all of this because I've either experienced it or I am experiencing it right now.

In most places of the world, young and looking young is very important to women and to men; however the focus is on women. Woman aren't supposed to have wisdom lines (better known as winkles) because everyone wants a smooth face.

Well, I've lived a lot of life and each winkle has a wonderful memory or event behind it and I like my wisdom lines.

Let's ask some questions about why we're so obsessed with this age, beauty and body stuff and see what comes up. After all, if we live forever, what does it matter? Let's try to remember that being human is an honor and we should honor our bodies because they carry us to wherever we want to go. It's like a car, if you want to go someplace you put gas in it, not sugar.

Well, our bodies are like a car. If we put cheat gas in it, it won't run well. If we put sugar in the gas tank, it breaks down. If we don't change the tires when they are worn out, we get a flat and need help fixing it. Regular tune ups and oil changes keep it running better and longer. Isn't it great we have visual metaphors for everything! Who thought of this? Just look around and be conscious about things and you'll see how many things are metaphors for us.

The body is a wonderful working machine and we need to take care of it, however we do get carried away once in awhile. You can go from one extreme or another on anything and our thoughts about how to look good fit right into all this extreme thinking.

Today there are hundreds and thousands of anti-wrinkle creams, firming creams, anti-aging creams, pills to make you look younger, thinner and almost anything else you might want. Beauty and anti-aging is a multi-billion dollar industry!

Everyone has a different thought about age, beauty and body stuff and how they view them. Some people like thin people and some like fatter people. Some like blondes and some like brunettes. Everyone has an opinion and a favorite and that's great. But as with anything, obsession is not a good thing.

When we're in our energy body, there are no wrinkles or body stuff. We don't age or get fatter or thinner or have gray hair or become bald. We are pure energy. I feel this is why we are so age conscious when we're in the human body. We just aren't used to aging.

Here's my take on it. Each Earth lifetime lasts about 75 to 100 years. We can stay on the other side any where from 1 day to 1000 years before we reincarnate. Because we don't age on the other side, we just forget it happens on this side.

If you ask anyone over the age of 60 how old they feel, most will tell you they feel 35 years old. When I get in touch with souls on the other side, most of them have gone back to 35 years old. Now if we are billions of years old, how can we not feel it? Because we are energy and we are consistently renewing our energy.

Creating is the renewing force. How do you feel when you create something? Don't you feel like you have accomplished something? Don't you feel pride in what you did? Don't you feel calm, complete and relaxed? This is the renewing energy of creating.

The duality of the Universe works like this – we put out energy to create and the same amount of energy we put out is returned to us so we can recharge and renew. Even if it's a big project and we have to rest, we are letting the energy renew its self so we can create again. It's a wonderful thing.

Ever notice people who do nothing or very little are always the ones who are tired? I'm not saying everyone has or should have the same energy level, but I feel the more we create in a positive way, the more positive energy we get back. It has to do with the main rule of the Universe – "what you put out, you get back."

Creating negatively creates negative results. When you put out positive energy, positive energy will return to you and recharge your batteries. Negative is always in the minus category and positive is always in the plus. See even our math is a metaphor for our lives.

In this time of "ageless" beauty products we need to remember that nothing will stop us from aging. It's the way this Universe and the human body works. Just like the flowers that come up in the spring, blossom and then die, we too are in that circle of life.

We can go have face lifts, tummy tucks, boob jobs, butt jobs, suck the fat out of places and whatever else you can think of but we can't stop the aging process from the inside of our bodies. We can look twenty on the outside forever, but the inside organs will always be aging. Why is this?

I believe because our soul lives forever, we don't need "bodies" to live forever. If our human body lived forever, we would have to be on Earth forever and when the sun burns out in 5 billions years, what would we do?

As humans we might not be equipped to handle space or other planets. So it's a good thing we don't live forever as humans. Besides we need to go home and regenerate our energy after about 100 years here on Earth. Earth is hard on our human body as well as our energy body.

Earth's energy is hard on our energy bodies because of the different pulls of gravity and energies we run into every day. These outside energies can age our bodies and deplete our energy. We might not even feel these energies but they are constant and our energy bodies deal with them 24/7.

Everyone knows as we age, we get shorter because of the lifelong pull of gravity on our bodies, and this pull adds to our aging process. It pulls on our skin, bones and muscles all the time. We don't even think about it but our energy body and human body are very aware of this pull. If we were on the moon, we probably wouldn't have as many wrinkles. Or we might not get wrinkles until we are in our seventies.

But we do live on Earth with different energies so we have to face the fact we will age. Everything in this Universe and all universes age or we wouldn't have black holes and burnt out suns. Like I said in the beginning – the only promise is we, our souls, will live forever, nothing more, nothing less.

That's almost too much for us to wrap our heads around. We think if we look younger we're some how going to stay younger or live longer, not true. You're only as old as you feel in your head, not in your body. Even if you have an illness or other body functions that seem to hold you back, your thinking doesn't have to be old. I know hundreds of people in their 80's and older that still do what they want and think young.

My grandmother thought she was old at 40 and developed Alzheimer's, which she died from. My dad was so afraid he'd do the same thing, he swore he'd never grow old. He is now 85 and is just starting to slow down but his brain is very much there. He has his health problems but he still does what he can, when he can and that's keeps him young and going. He and my mom still traveled up until a couple of months ago. They live independently however this last year, my dad's health is starting to fail, but not his mind.

I know there are some things we can't change but just because our parents had something go wrong with them, doesn't mean we have to buy into the idea it will happen to us.

Buying into any thought form or energy means we start to believe it and become it. I've always wondered if we could eat cake and not gain a pound if no one ever told us it was fattening. If no one told us we had to get old, would we? If we didn't know that our bodies start to age the second we are born, would we even consider dying one day? If no one told us death was the "unknown" and we just knew one day we would leave our bodies and go home, would we fear death?

Look at all the stories, thought forms and ideas we buy into and we don't even know if they're the truth or a big fat lie. Wow, no wonder we live in fear all the time. Aging is normal for the human body, plants, and animals and rocks. It's just not going to last forever. So why are we so obsessed with staying young?

The answer is because we don't age on the other side. We never grow old on the other side. If we don't grow old there, we don't understand why we have to do it here. It's the same principle as we only have love on the other side when we are in the Light, so when we get here, all we want is love and can't seem to find it.

Love is already in us and around us but our human body doesn't feel this "love vibration" like our energy body does. Want to know why? Love is an intangible energy vibration that our energy body feels more than the human body.

Our human body wants to be held and touched physically but our energy body doesn't need that. It's already sensitive to the energy of love and every other energy on Earth. However, just like our cars need a good wax rubbed into the paint to keep them protected and shiny, we need rubbed and touched to feel the energy of love.

Humans require a lot of touching because they have tuned out their energy body and they don't know how to relate to anything else. They have to be touched to feel accepted and loved. It's just like "looking good". We need someone to tell us we "look good" to make us "feel good".

But Earth is not a beauty school; it's a learning and growing school. We have taught everyone for the last ten thousand years or so that beauty is in the eyes of the beholder but then we turn right around and say it's only beautiful if it's young. If beauty is in the eyes of the beholder, then there is no ugly. Ugly is an ugly word. It sounds ugly and it's spelled ugly. I think we need to take it out of our vocabulary. We should just say, "I like it or I don't like it." Being ugly is like having cancer in this society. No one wants to look at you or acknowledge you. And who are we to say what's ugly and what's not.

The fact remains our society is too focus on what the perfect woman and man should look like. Are we so mesmerized by sex, boobs and penises we are losing the true meaning of their purpose?

Sex is a way of keeping our species going – yes, it can be something just to enjoy but it shouldn't be the main focus for living. If you really dug into all the pheromones, psychology, blood flood and other bodily functions that have to happen just to want or perform sex, it would turn you off. Yet we are so focused on it because long ago we were told it was mysterious and forbidden.

There are many cultures around the world that still view sex as just another body function. It's not a big deal; it's just part of life and the continuation of life. In many countries religions have put the fear of God in us when it comes to sex. They think there is something un-natural or dirty about it. This kind of thinking has made sex very mysterious for many and they view it more on the dark side then on the Light side of things.

Sex used to represent the union of a man and woman, or in the time of the Lemurians it was the masculine and feminine energy coming together to create something. Sex was also a very sacred event between a man and a woman and I think this is why we still make a big deal of it. I also think as humans, we feel like we aren't connected to anyone on this side unless we have sex with them.

So being told that sex is dirty or some "thing" you can't have unless you're married or living with someone, otherwise it's a sin, has been engrained in us for thousands of years. This is where another human condition comes in to play.

Have you ever noticed its human nature to want something you can't have? Ever watch someone try and get something he wants even if he knows it's not going to be good for him? Doesn't everyone try to get what they don't have?

If you want to see someone make an ass out of himself, just tell him he can't have it. A human will do almost anything to get an object he wants; be it a mate or a free ticket to something. He'll try even harder if someone tells him he can't have it. People will make excuses, lie or even beg to get something someone else told them they can't have. It's sad but true.

Then they get it and what happens? We don't want it! We lose interest. How many times have you wanted to jump into bed with someone only to find the fantasy was a hundred times better than the reality?

Sex is sex and stop thinking it's some kind of "cure-all" or something that will make a difference in your life.

The only thing that makes a difference in your life is love. Sex and love are not the same thing. Sex is like a good sneeze. There's a build up and then a release and it's over. Love is something that grows with time and you feel it all the time.

Sex is quick and gone.

When the sex is gone, we start looking for something to remind us of the sex – whether it was good or not. We are very visual creatures so we start looking for something that will entice us into thinking sex with someone else might be better. Men look for bigger or better boobs or butts. Women look for muscles, butts and penises.

It only takes a day or two to forget a bad "one night stand" and then we're at looking for another one. Haven't we learned our lesson about one night stands? They're either not that good or someone gets hurt.

It's dumb but then again we can't stand it when someone with big boobs or a large bulge in the front of his pants walks through the door. We aren't looking at them; we're looking at body parts. The visual affects of what the bumps in their cloths might look like starts the old sex engine and we forget all about last night and how quickly a fantasy can turn into a nightmare. So we end up with someone new, another one nighter and more disappointment.

We have been bombarded with so much sex on TV, radio, stage and everywhere we turn, we think if we aren't interested in sex, there's something wrong with us. Our sub-conscious picks up all the ads and songs and then plays it back to us over and over again until we are not only believing it, we're living it.

Well, sex is over rated and as with any relationship, when you get old enough not to care about sex, you better have a lot of love there to keep the relationship going. There is a certain age when the body is not beautiful anymore and then love better be able to get you through.

All too soon big boobs are not perky any more and you're just trying to keep them out of your lap. And speaking of laps, the bulge in the pants will shrivel too. I can remember my dad saying, "As you get older, you shrink. As a matter of fact, everything shrinks. You'd think because a penis hangs down, gravity would pull on it and it would get bigger, but it doesn't."

I about wet my pants laughing at him.

Why do we want to have or see the prefect boobs anyway? What are the prefect boobs? Is it a C or D cup or maybe a A cup is right? Who knows? Who cares? Boobs are supposed to be used to feed children.

Believe it or not, there are a lot of places around the world where a woman's chest isn't important. Many cultures view a breast as just something a woman uses for nursing. I think because we live in a country where the mentality is "bigger is better" for fast food meals, we think boobs need to be bigger too.

And while we're on the subject of "bigger"; what about penises? It would be well to remember that a vaginal opening and canal has only so much room. Yes it can stretch but like any thing else, "too much of a good thing may not be a good thing."

What is it with everything has to be bigger or the biggest? I'd much rather have a partner who cares for me deeply than to be in me too deeply.

Then we have the face lifts; here's what happens. You get a face lift and look younger but the skin will always continue to age. So if you want to stay wrinkle free, you have to get another one and another one. Soon you're looking like Joan Rivers whose face is pulled so tight she has a permanent smile and her nose looks like it could have been her belly button.

There's no way right now to stop the aging process. We're supposed to age. We're supposed to die. We're supposed to come back and do it again and again. Look at nature and get the lesson of life, death and rebirth. Everything on Earth and in this Universe does this. Why are we so surprised about it? Why do we think we don't have to do it? We have to follow the rules of the Universe, no matter what Universe we're in.

Now I've heard that Moses lived 900 years and that might be possible but what was a year back then? We know the Mayans used two calendars. One had 365 days which was called a vague year. The other calendar had 260 days and called a sacred year.

So what was considered a year in Moses' time? What I'm trying to get across is that in this Universe with the rules and laws that run it, everything starts to die as soon as it's born or spouts. This is what this Universe is all about.

In many cultures around the world, the elders are looked up too with respect. Their age is a sign of wisdom. I don't see that in the United States – I see little respect for anything and a lot of greed for everything.

We're all striving for that prefect "something". We can't seem to get it on this side and we don't know why. It might be because of the duality we live in. Whatever we have on this side, we don't have on the other side and visa versa. So if we have only love and perfection on the other side of the death veil, we might not be able to get it here. It's like if we are energy on the other side, we have to be solid here. Duality is something we really need to think about and remember it's probably bigger than any of us understand.

Perfect is only what you think it is and becoming that perfect someone shouldn't have anything to do with physical beauty. Becoming perfect should have to do with your energy system.

Another thing to think about is the probability we have already been both a man and a woman in one life time or another. We just can't remember all of our life times and everything we did, which is a good thing. I often think about this and, for all I know, I could have been a one eyed-Cyclops in one of my life times – now there's a plastic surgeon's night-mare.

Some of us might have already had the life time where we were the most perfect man or woman in a physical form so we don't need to experience that again. Also we need to remember that ideas change with every generation. What was considered perfect 20 years ago might be rejected in today's world. Change is what keeps us moving and nothing is set in stone.

When we reach a certain age, and that age is different for everyone, we start to realize beauty and body stuff doesn't matter much. Even sex is not the most important thing on the planet after you've been here awhile.

My mother is 82 and a great lady. She doesn't much care about sex or how she looks in a bathing suit any more. She's just glad to wake up in the morning and still be breathing. That doesn't mean she doesn't care how she looks because she does. It's just not the most important thing in the world.

She has this great saying, "If someone doesn't like the way I look, they can look the other way."

On this side of the veil of death, as so many call it, there's a belief if we just stay young and pretty we'll live forever. Somehow being younger and prettier will keep the "'ol wolf from the door". Nothing will keep age and death from your door. When it's your time, it's your time.

The only people that seem to stay young are the movie stars that have died young. We see them in a movie and they never get any older. Movie stars spend a lot of time on looking good and if you want to do that, it's okay. I have better things to do. I feel if I eat right, move my energy in a positive way and help people, I'll stay young from the inside out.

I'm okay with me but I can't wait until I get to where my mother is with her thinking. She eats what she wants too, goes where she wants too, buys what she wants too, and has a great time because she doesn't worry what others will think of her. If you really think about it, getting to that "perfect body" might just mean getting to the age of being comfortable with your body no matter what it looks like.

If you were the only person on Earth, you'd be pretty happy with yourself just the way you are but because humans are very visual creatures, we look at someone else and want to either be like them or better than they are somehow.

If no one told you how pretty or ugly you were, how would you know? If commercials told us it was sexy to be over-weight and have pimples on our faces, we would lust after that look I'm sure. Commercials play on the radio and TV so much they start to become part of our subconscious; and as we all know, our subconscious runs our life.

We need to have commercials that tell us we're fine just the way we are. We need to be told we're beautiful and nothing's wrong with any of us.

I believe we're obsessed with beauty and looks because in our energy body we are beautiful. We have a natural glow and we're very good looking – all of us. We'll like angels and you'll never see a bad looking angel. This is why I think we're so worried about the way we look when we're in the human body.

We made a contract with ourselves to come to Earth to learn lessons and the only way to learn them is through the type of body we choose. Look at your body and then at your life. There is always a connection with these two things and the contract you came here to fulfill.

While we're on the subject of contracts, I'd like to insert something here. The contract is only between you and yourself. Our spirit guides and angels help us make it up on the other side before we incarnate but it's not "with" anyone but you. You have decided what you what to learn this time by meeting the people you meet and doing the things you do.

If you really look at the human body, it's not pretty no matter how much plastic surgery you've done. I mean look very closely at just one small spot on your arm and you'll understand what I'm saying. There's usually dead, dry skin with tiny lines running every which way. You can see small holes in the skin which are our pores but they have hair growing out of them. Really look at your body and you'll be glad you don't have to look at it that closely all the time. Besides, beauty fits into the illusion category. Beauty is not a tangible thing so it has to be an illusion. What happens to illusions? They fade away.

Could it be we are so obsessed with body stuff because this is the only Universe we've been in where there are so many differences in each body? If you read about people who have seen aliens, most of them describe aliens as looking the same. One might be an inch or two shorter or taller but they're basic description is the same.

Not so with humans. Every human looks totally different from the next one unless you're a twin.

Could it be that because we CAN change our looks, we just want too? Wouldn't this be part of creating something? We are creating how we look just like we create how we act, think and speak.

Changing our outward appearance can and does change how we think about ourselves therefore it changes how we act too. I once knew a lady who was very over-weight. She had a gastric operation so she could control her eating and lose weight. Well, she did lose weight but then other men starting noticing her. Her husband was still very over-weight and she started losing interest in him.

He didn't have the energy she now had and he didn't give her the attention the other men were giving her. Their divorce was quick and he was devastated. He had loved her for who she had been, not for what her body looked like. When she lost the weight, she became a different person.

As humans we identify with what we see, smell, taste and touch. We can't do all these things on the other side so we experience them here. When we change our surrounds or body, our perception of everything changes. It's like moving from one country to another. There maybe trees that look like the ones back home but the language is different, the people do things differently and we change and adjust so we can be part of it.

So before you decide to get rebuilt, pumped up, sucked out or tightened up, think about how it's going to affect you and others around you. If you are doing it because it will give you more self-confidence, stop and think about this. If you find more self-confidence from something fake or that's not you, then your self-confidence is fake and not really you either. Look deep inside and pull out who you are before you make-up something you're not.

From boobs to facelifts to feelings, if it's not part of who you are in the beginning, it will never be truly who you really are after the operations. We all have to look deep inside ourselves to pull out our true self because just like you can't judge a book by its' cover, you can't judge a human by their looks. If you have fake looks and fake feelings then you might be attracting fake friends.

I think a sex change operation is great because if you're a male and there's a female inside of you, then the female is really who you are. Situations like that are important so a person can feel like themselves. If you were born with a deformed lip or nose and need surgery to correct it, then do it. There are millions of reasons to have work done but doing it for an "ego" reason shouldn't be one of them.

I have a friend who has implants in her breasts. She has noticed that one of them seems to be getting smaller and she knows she probably has a leak in the implant. As she was telling me this, she said something I'd like to share with you.

She said, "I'm going to have both of the implants removed. I'm done with them. Anyway, I think they attract the wrong kind of men. I want someone who will look into my face and not my chest."

I gave her a big hug because she had learned a very good lesson. She learned the men she was attracting were more interested in her body and body parts then in her and what she was all about. She's a very pretty woman with or without her implants and that won't change.

I'm not saying it's wrong to look good. But what's looking good? Who's the judge?

I believe if someone wants to change everything about their body, then do it, just look at the reasons you're doing it before you do it. Don't let it become an obsession.

I had some work done on my face years ago because one of my eyes was sagging from the eye socket being broken when my ex-husband hit me in one of his many drunken rages. After the surgery it not only looked better but it made me "see" better. If you want to look younger than do it, but don't do it every other year. Know who you are before you change it.

I think at my age, I now feel okay with myself. I have many wisdom lines, not wrinkles. I'm two inches shorter than I was at 25 and it had to go somewhere, so it went to my waist. My breasts have never been big but I'm now thankful because they aren't sagging and I can still go without a bra if I want too. My legs and butt are still in good shape because I walk a lot.

I feel I have my mother's genes and she is still a looker at 82 - so I have a few more good years in me. But here again, all of this is from my eyes, my prospective. What I really like is I can now sit back and look in the mirror and tell myself "I love you just the way you are." And that's a good feeling.

If we can try to look at everyone with love and accept them for who they are, we'll over look most of the physical things that could be considered "flaws". Flaws are things we can learn from and embrace if we just look past them to the true nature or meaning of them.

Several hundred or even thousands of years ago we weren't worried about our looks so much. Maybe we didn't care about our looks because we didn't have as many mirrors as we do now. Or it might be that the mirrors were so distorted back then they didn't give us a good image of ourselves anyway. Or could it be they just accepted people for who they were and the way they looked because they hadn't been told what was beautiful and what wasn't.

Back then everyone had hairy legs, hairy arm pits and hair in places I don't want to think about. No one worried about body odor, hair lice or dirt because everyone had them. People were dirty and that's the way it was. People were more worried about surviving every day. There was disease, war and many other things that were more important than our looks. Heck, many of us didn't even bath for months or even years at a time.

We now have more time on our hands and because we're in a pretty stable environment, our common sense just goes right out the window. Do you think many people in Iran or other warring countries worry about how big their boobs or penises are? I bet if you asked them they'd tell you they're just happy to be alive with all their body parts still attached.

We need to realize age and beauty go hand in hand and everyone can be beautiful at any age. We are timeless, ageless beings in spirit and we have to experience time and age to really appreciate what we have on the other side.

Here's an exercise we did in psychic school that you might try.

You stand in front of a full length mirror naked every morning and look at the image you see and say, "I love you just the way you are." Its fun and soon you start loving you for you. Once you learn to do that, you can love someone else for who they are.

Besides, if we all had long, thick lashes, smooth skin, manageable hair with no gray in it, long shapely legs, big boobs or penises, no body fat and well defined muscles, no dry skin, no oily skin, no pimples or flaws on our faces, were all about 5' 6" to 6' and tan with no tan lines, we'd soon get bored at looking at ourselves and each other.

I remember my ex-husband telling me that if he had boobs he's never leave the house because he would be playing them all the time. Well, now he's in he's sixties and has man boobs. I couldn't resist asking him if he goes out or is he too busy playing with his chest. He shot me a dirty look and I got him a 42 D bra for Christmas a few years ago. He's still not speaking to me.

When we are in the human body, we have a brain we use for most of our daily activities. When we are in the energy body, we don't have a brain, vocal cords, hands, arms, feet and really no other body parts. Wow, so how do we function? What is that like?

Being out of body is something our brain has trouble with. How can we possibly do anything without body parts? Well let's take it one part at a time.

We don't have a physical brain so how do we think? Our energy body stores every emotion and energy feeling we have ever had in all our life times. That's a lot of information but its information we need and use. We can call on it every time we are here as long as we understand it's there for the taking. It's getting to the point of knowing we all have more knowledge than we think that's the hard part.

We don't have a brain in the energy body or Spirit so we have to think things into reality using our energy. Thoughts are energy but we don't need a brain to "think". On the other side souls send us energy waves that hit our bodies and then waves are sent to our brain to understand. It's like the bottom of our foot starts to itch and the nerve tells our brain to scratch it.

Really if we didn't have a brain in the human body to tell us what to do, our body would just stop functioning. Our energy body is different. It transfers messages through energy.

I can remember when I was watching my body die from the other side. Every time I had a thought about what the paramedics were doing to my body, they answered like I was next to them asking the question. It was strange and yet I somehow knew on a soul level, they could hear me.

We don't have to "eat" when we are in the energy body. We "eat" by picking up more energy. We really just absorb it into our energy body. I'm not sure how that works but when I was on the other side, I felt great and I actually remember having a lot of energy in my body

157

within a couple of hours. I didn't want to stay in the hospital but they made me.

Because we're all energy, we just have to "want" to do something and we can manifest it out of thin air, so to speak. When we are in our energy body, we know the secrets of the universe, which aren't really secrets once we get to the other side. We form things with energy and if we want to live in a house we can or we can just be "free spirits" and travel. We don't need sleep but we do need to rest sometimes and renew our energy.

All of this is very hard to understand because we have to relate things to "body stuff" on this side. Everything on the other side relates to "energy" so it works very differently and we can't understand that when we are in the human body. Because humans are very visual, we really have to see something to believe it, right? That's why we all want to see a ghost or spirit to make sure they really exist.

On the other side, we experience and keep learning about how to work with and create with energy. Over here we learn how to work and create with physical things. It's really all energy but our energy is frozen or slower moving then the energy on the other side. The energy of Earth has different rules than the energy of Mars, Venus or any other planet. That's already been proven.

So if we can learn on both sides, why do so many of us choose to come back again and again? Isn't life hard enough? Why would we want to repeat it over and over again? Well, there are many reasons but I think a big one is the addiction we all have to food.

We can manifest food on the other side but it's not the same because we don't have taste buds. Wow, I'm beginning to think I don't want to go home and miss out on fried chicken, tomatoes right from the garden, hot home-made bread and chocolate! Maybe this should be the main reason not to commit suicide too.

I'm sure when we're on the other side things are great and we love it there but humans love the taste of food too. If you really think about it, food is a very large part of life on this planet. The animal kingdom is an "eat or be eaten" world. And even vegetarians are killing plants to eat them. So the whole planet is about food and survival. I know that's not a pretty thought but it's true.

This whole planet is about living and dying. That's what everything on Earth does in one form or another. That's really all there is – life, learning and dying. A hundred years from now no one will remember if you had a wart on your finger, your nose or any where else. No one will care. It's really about how you lived your life and what you learned.

Your body is only a vehicle to move your soul around. However, you want to keep your body in good running condition so you can go more places and experience more things. It doesn't matter how big your boobs are because in the scheme of things, boobs don't mean a thing.

When we leave the human body, we'll understand it's only a place we inhabited to help us learn about this universe and all its wonders. The next universe will be different and have different things to learn and experience. The body is important to keep fit and running well but size doesn't matter on any part of our body, just like color doesn't matter.

We have to experience different ethnic groups to understand why there are different groups. We have to be rich, poor, a man, a woman and so many other things in different life times just to learn what it's like. We come back to learn, to heal, to share and to experience life as only it can exist here on this planet. Earth is the only one of its kind, at least in this solar system. We don't know about other solar systems and what they might hold for us.

What it all boils down too is experiencing and learning. That's all. It's a simple master plan. Five hundred years from now no one will care or even remember, except you and you'll smile because you learned something.

So look in the mirror and tell yourself you love you! You created the body your in for a reason. Sure you can now reshape it, remake and do lots of things to it, but do it for a good reason. Remember, once you change the outside, many times you change the inside. Why not start with the inside and work your way out? Just bringing in the Light of love and caring can make you more attractive.

So let's lighten up on the body and aging stuff and pay more attention to what's really important – ice cream!

Understanding Our Ageless Creative Energies

Where did the first humans come from? The Earth? The sky? From God? What is creative energy? How do we use this energy as humans? How do we use it as energy beings?

These are questions we are just starting to ask and may one day find the answers but as for now, we sit and ponder the answers. There are many people studying the past and each one seems to have their own theory on things so the following is just that - a theory. It's a theory about energy, the human body and how or why all of this came about.

When the Lemurians were on Earth, some people believe they were neither masculine or feminine but carried both energies in their bodies; the same as we do today. These energies have nothing to do with mating only with creating. That got me wondering if or how Lemurians mated or multiplied or even if they had too. I thought about this and then I asked my spirit guides to help me with the answers, this is what I heard.

When Lemurians were first coming to Earth, everything was energy including the them. They numbered in the billions because they were really just souls floating around this solar system learning about creation. Many of us were probably Lemurians and were hanging around this universe watching it being formed.

All these shape-shifting Lemurian souls came and went as they pleased. They didn't need to be born as we know it because they were already alive. They just came to Earth and then went back to wherever they came from. The gravitational pull on the Earth wasn't what it is today and so they had free run of it, so to speak.

The birthing process of all souls had already taken place billions of years before when the creative power made all of us. Since our creator had already made us, there was no need to be "born". We already were alive, just in a different form.

As the gravitational pull became greater and greater, as we stated before, energies started to get "stuck" and frozen. Once this started to happen, the Lemurians couldn't continue their free lifestyle and something had to be done.

The Lemurians' masculine and feminine energies had to work together to create something. This was how things were created. Each Lemurian knew they could just think about something and it would manifest if they put enough energy into it. They would think it, plan it, put energy into it and then move toward making it happen, which is called taking action. This is the birthing process.

Lemurians birthed experiences into reality. This would relate back to the holo-deck we talked about in the "Illusion" chapter. So their birthing process was to create things they could experience here on Earth. Because there was already billions of them, they didn't have a need to birth babies. If they wanted to come to Earth, they just flew down and landed.

As the gravitational pull of Earth got heavier and the Lemurians got stuck here, manifesting creations and experiences became harder. Souls couldn't just come into the heavier energy and play. There had to be a way to continue to bring souls to Earth to experience life in a different way.

They realized their energy vibration was higher than Earth's and they either couldn't stay here long or if they lowered their vibration to match that of the planets', they got stuck here. They had already experienced being animals and plants by shape-shifting into them. They had learned how they mated or reproduced. It was fascinating to them because as Lemurians, they didn't need a seed or egg to create something. They used energy.

They were finding it was taking more and more effort to create something from nothing when on the planets' surface. They also realized they needed a vehicle of some kind they could be in to protect their energy and kept them on the planet. Some people think this was the beginning of the human body.

They realized the human body had to have some of the elements of Earth so it would match the vibration of the planet and be able to survive. Some people think this is where God said to the Lemurians, "Let's make man (humans) in our images."

It took a lot of work to create the human body we have now and we're still working on perfecting it. So far most of the human skeletons that have been found from the past are very much like we are today. There are some differences but that's just evolution which is also a natural occurrence here on Earth. Evolution is also part of creating something new.

We still need to work on the body because it has parts that give out or need replaced or parts we can simply do without. The body is an amazing piece of work but far from perfect. We are still working on "getting it right" even today. We can see the process of perfecting the human body in what science is doing with DNA and genes today. They're trying to make the prefect baby or end disease before it starts.

So the Lemurians had to become human but not without their problems. The human body made a great carrier for the soul which meant the soul could still create and manifest thru it, however, there was still one problem they needed to solve. How were other souls going to enter Earth's heavier atmosphere? The ever changing energy on Earth was a challenge but the Lemurians knew there had to be a way to bring more souls to Earth. Because they had experience the birthing process of plants and animals, they had to figure a way to reproduce the human form. They couldn't just call on God every time a soul wanted to come to Earth. He was way to busy for that.

They couldn't just fall from the sky anymore either. Everything had shifted on Earth and you needed a human body or some kind of body to stay on the planet. Energy "beings" couldn't just jump into objects or other beings anymore. The vibration of life on Earth was to slow for them to do that anymore. The Lemurians couldn't stay on Earth as an energy "being" because their vibration was too high. This meant they had to find a way to slow down their energy so they could enter a body and stay here.

This meant a whole new way of life for the Lemurians. They realized they couldn't just slow their vibration down in a few seconds and expect it to stay that way. Lower their vibrational energy was not a natural thing for them to do. Because, once it was lowered, they were no longer energy beings and had to be "in" something to keep it lower. It would take some practice to lower their vibration and keep it at this lower state.

What they found was it took about eight to nine Earth months to be able to lower their vibration and keep it at the lower rate. They also needed to get used to a human body a little at a time because it was so different from the energy body their were used too. It was like putting on a suit of armor. It was heavy and took a lot of energy to function in one. They had to have a period of time when they could work on coming and going into the human form without exploding the human body with their higher vibration.

They also needed a place for the body to reside while they were lowering their vibration. A body couldn't just walk around without a soul in it. Thus the Lemurians took their two energies, the masculine and the feminine, and divided them to form a man and woman. The man would give the seed of humanness to the woman and the woman would nurture it and watch it grow. The woman would be the safe place a body could grow right along with a soul who was lowering his vibration to fit into that body. Thus the human carrier was created and now worked outwardly in the physical world like the two inward energies did in the Lemurians; both creating physical things. The eight to nine month incubation period was perfect for them. They visited the body of the unborn human everyday and began the process of lowering their vibration a little at a time.

There were many other things they had to adjust too as well. The human body was undergoing radical changes during this time. This is because the Lemurians were still learning what the human body needed to survive.

The Lemurians were all telepathic and didn't need vocal cords, just like we don't need them when we are in our energy bodies. However, the Lemurians soon found that telepathic thoughts moved much slower in the heavy energy of Earth than they did in the outer space arena of no gravity. Because thoughts are energy and the energy of Earth was getting heavier, thoughts were also getting heavier and moved slower.

So there needed to be another way of communication. Vocal cords began to evolve in the human body. Speaking and making sounds moved easier through the energy on Earth. Sounds have a different energy and vibration than telepathic energy and they just work better with Earth's vibration.

The Lemurians had to also figure out what they needed to eat to keep the body alive. After all, they had lived on energy for so long they didn't know how to "eat" solid food.

They had to learn about hot, cold, disease and all the other problems we encounter when we are in the human body. These were are learning, growing and creating experiences. All these experience helped to create the bodies we have today.

The Lemurians learned something about the human brain too; it only records things that happen in its' life time. It doesn't come with the memories of any past lives. These memories are stored in our energy bodies and we need experiences of some kind to bring them forward so our brain can recall them for us.

These experiences can be when we go some place and it seems familiar to us or we think we've been there before. That type of feeling will poke at the memory stored in our energy body so it will be delivered to our brain. Our brain doesn't remember the event or place; it's just being the messenger for the energy body. So by creating experiences, we remember the past and bring that knowledge forward from our energy body to our brain to help us with problems we may have in this life.

The Lemurians started this process tens of thousands of years ago and we are still doing it today. It's the only way to get all our memories of past lives to come forward to help us in the present. I can only imagine what we go through to come to this planet. I wish we could remember the other side better when we're here but then I guess we wouldn't learn as much, would we.

As Earth continued to grow and change, it's gravity was changing the flow of energy and how things functioned on the planet. With all these changes, the Lemurians had to change with it. This meant if they stayed an energy "being" they were had to be in a completely different energy dimension then Earth beings. This was the division of energy verses solid form. To really function on Earth and be part of Earth, you couldn't be all energy. The veil between dimensions was falling fast.

This was also the start of dividing the energies that had worked together for so long. No one could foresee what would happen when these two balanced energies were divided and had to stand on their own two feet, so to speak. The masculine energy was a given energy but also had the power to control or to take life away. The feminine energy was a nurturing energy but also had the choice not to nurture and to let things die. With humans evolving and Lemurians dying out, what would happen to the world. After all, as humans we don't feel connected to anything or anyone most of the time.

Now while I was thinking about all of this, the following fairytale came to mind to help explain the masculine and feminine energies. It's a story about how humans have misused these energies but it's also a story of hope and a return to balance.

The fairy tale starts out by giving you a simple explanation of what the two energies do and how they work together. Nothing can be created in this universe without these two energies working together.

The masculine energy is a giving energy. Whether it's the initial energy of a thought of rain, heat or the DNA encased in a seed, it's the energy that's necessary to start a project, to create or to give direction to something.

The feminine energy is of receiving and expanding. It's the energy that makes things happen, that transforms a thought into reality. It takes time to process and is often difficult and requires overcoming obstacles.

So when we get an idea, we nurture it and then bring it forward into reality. This is the feminine and masculine working together to form something new. The birth of this creation is always greater than both the energies but is impossible without either energy.

Now here's the fairy tale entitled "His-story, Her-story = the Missed-story" (mystery)

Once upon a time, long, long ago there was a planet in a Universe which had formed from a great explosion. This planet would later be known as Earth. It was a beautiful planet with balanced energy which supported all kinds of life. This balanced energy was important to all the functions and creations on Earth.

There was a soft, nurturing feminine energy to help things grow and there was a stronger masculine energy which gave strength to the feminine energy. The feminine could call on the masculine and the masculine could call on the feminine. This balance was known to every living thing on Earth.

Neither was the boss or the strongest; both were equal. Both needed each other to grow and survive. This was a time of joy, peace and creation. Father Sky gave Mother Earth the rain and sun to help her grow things on the planet.

There was a lot of life on Earth but most of it was either very small or very big. It took millions of years but one day a race of humans seemed to fall from the sky. The Earth knew and understood it took two energies working together to accomplish anything on its' surface. The humans watched the Earth and how things were created. They began to understand there was a masculine energy and feminine energy that worked together to manifest everything. They knew these two energies worked like the energies they carried in their bodies. There was no bad, evil or judgment about these energies. They were accepted as part of life and the balance life needed to stay healthy.

But soon things started to change. Many humans began to question these energies and wondered if they were both needed to create things. They were beginning to mistrust these energies and thought humanness might be more powerful than these energies. This was the beginning of the shadow of darkness. This shadow was hiding in the dark areas of the humans' brain, watching the masculine and feminine energies with envy. It was the Big Bad Ego, lurking in the forest of the human mind and he was planning an attack. He wanted to capture the masculine energy. He thought if he could conquer the masculine his could control the feminine because he viewed her as weak.

He waited and planned his attack. It had to be at the right time. Timing would be everything because he lived in the consciousness of all humans. This consciousness was new and there were many things to learn. He knew because of the newness there would be the fear of the unknown and he was counting on this fear to work in his favor. He would have to wait until the humans were so fearful they would listen and believe his lies about the feminine being a weak link. He would have to get the humans to trust him not themselves.

He watched and waited until the time was right. He jumped out of the dark forest of the human consciousness and pushed the masculine away from the feminine. There was only a brief struggle because without the support of each other, both the masculine and the feminine energies were out of balance.

The Big Bad Ego took control of the masculine energy and this is where the story of "oneness" and "together" changed; it became "me & I". This was the beginning of fear and Imbalance became a partner in crime with the Big Bad Ego.

This was also the beginning of his-story as told by man in his fear, not by our Creator. It said the feminine was not part of the masculine and should be left behind because of her weakness. This was the beginning of the missed-story.

Natural healers, witches, warlocks and shamans all had balanced energies at this time and knew the feminine was in trouble. The balance had to be restored so the mystical, magical ways of the Universe could continue. They tried to keep the balance but the Big Bad Ego was separating the masculine more and more every day.

As the Big Bad Ego gained more power over the masculine, more wars and hatred spread throughout the land. The Big Bad Ego was playing with the people like they were string puppets. With each new war Imbalance grew stronger. The healers were losing their fight to keep the energies balanced.

Power became the main goal instead of nurturing and growth. The Big Bad Ego's partner, Imbalance, raised his nasty head and huffed and puffed until the feminine was all but blown away.

When this happened, Imbalance quickly spread his campaign of jealousy, untrustworthiness and deceit throughout the land. The Big Bad Ego had started taking control of the many healers with his lies and promises of power and fame. They too began to ignore the feminine energy. She was becoming very weak. She couldn't even help the healers that still believed in her because of her weakness.

Then it happened, with one great swoop of the Big Bad Ego's thoughts and actions, the healers where done away with. This was done to protect the Big Bad Ego's lies. He was telling the masculine energy he didn't need the feminine anymore. The Big Bad Ego was very strong and the masculine gave in to him and his stories.

Once this happened, the Land of planet Earth was thrown completely out of balance. No longer did the masculine and feminine energies work together. The Big Bad Ego had control over the masculine energy and instead of giving, the masculine started taking. The more he took the more the feminine suffered. Finally she wasn't strong enough to fight and was forced into silence by the Big Bad Ego. The Big Bad Ego then ruled the out of balance masculine energy for many, many years.

Her-story tells us the feminine waited in silence. She needed to heal herself and gain strength. She was silent but knew there were many people who still felt her and had faith in her. She finally began to feel like Tinkerbelle in the story of Peter Pan, coming back to life.

All of these silent healers had been her eyes and ears of the world for thousands of years. They too were in silence, afraid of the Big Bad Ego but little by little they began to find each other and talk. They started to uncover the truth about the two energies needing each other. They were afraid they might suffer at the hands of the Big Bad Ego if he found them but the feminine energy assured them she was getting stronger everyday and told them not to worry. The time was coming when she and the masculine would be reunited to rule in balance.

It took many years but she finally regained enough strength and power to start planning a movement of her own. She was ready to reclaim her spot next to the masculine power. She started gathering followers with a force that couldn't be ignored.

Her-story finally began to surface. It's a story about how we need to nurture ourselves, each other and Earth. It's a story of bringing forward a birth greater than ourselves.

It's a story of how the "fairy godmother" we each have inside of ourselves can cast a loving spell on the Big Bad Ego and turn him into a silent toad. Then we can nurture him and when we're ready, we'll kiss him and turn him into the "handsome prince charming" that has balanced energy.

Together His-story and Her-story can uncover the Missed-story of life. The two are partners in purpose who unite to find the One within us. The Presence, the Oneness of these two energies that make up who we are, appears outwardly as man and woman, as yin and yang, in all of creation and in the entire Universe. It's the Law of the Land.

This Missed-story is from thousands of year of His-story telling us only the masculine view. Now it's time for His-story and Her-story to once again join hands, walking in balance to uncover the Missed-story and complete it with the only story; the never ending story of life, love and the purpose of us being here to live again and again and forever and ever.

To nurture and be nurtured, to grow strong and be strong and to love and be loved in a balanced way. That's what this fair tale is all about; to understand being human is just a fairy tale of what life actually is and to not let the Big Bad Ego eat us but to teach it how to feed us.

Life is the soul we carry around in this body that continues when the body dies. The fairy tale we are living is supposed to be a magical, mystical, wonderful, joyous story but too many people don't believe in fairy tales these days. Too many people believe in night mares and horror stories and that's how they live their lives.

Yet, behind every fairy tale or horror story there is a truth to uncover. Mother Earth and Father Sky show us these truths everyday. The flower that comes up, blossoms and then dies every year. Our DNA that tells us who we are and the truths of the Universe we can't ignore.

Once we start to balance the energies in us, we can start to again balance the energies outside of us. We can start in our life and our own back yards. None of us can change the world over night, but if we start with our own lives, we are really changing a small piece of the world.

Once the balance is restored, everyone can live happily ever after on this planet but that's just the beginning of another story.

Just like any fairy tale, there are some questions that come up. Some of the questions might be -

How would God, the masculine as many view him, know how to make the image of a woman or the feminine if wasn't an example to follow? Doesn't it make sense there had to be Goddess too? Or is the Creator both masculine and feminine and therefore the very balance we're looking for? Or did the Creator know we humans are so visual we needed a physical man and a physical woman to see the masculine and feminine energies and their purpose in life?

No matter what you think or believe, these energies are the energies of life on this planet and in this Universe. Once we understand them and bring them into balance in ourselves, we can create or manifest anything we really want. These energies might not be on another planet. This might be the only planet where there are different sexes, which brings us back to the last chapter and why we might be so obsessed with sex.

So before you get too carried away with sex and the male and female species of this planet, think about what they are really about. They are about the masculine or feminine energies that create and bring about "births" of new things. That's the real reason for them.

Look at them in depth because once we start to understand our ageless creative abilities, we just might use them to create better "things".

So the story goes that Lemurians began to birth other souls onto Earth and through this birthing process, our memories of who we are and why we came here began to get lost. Birth is a trauma to the soul, just like death is a trauma. This makes us forget some "things" as we cross over into different dimensions.

Many times we forget why we reincarnated back to Earth in the first place. Because our memories are stored in our energy bodies and not the human brain when we're in spirit form, some things will be pushed aside. Unimportant events might even be forgotten but they are never lost.

Events that aren't lessons or really have nothing to do with us might never be stored in our energy body because there is no need for them.

An example of this might be when the A-bomb was dropped on Japan in World War II. If you weren't alive in the world at this time, you probably won't have it stored in your energy body. It had nothing to do with you back then and it has nothing to do with you now. There's no reason your energy body needs to store it or even recall it, but if you were alive at that time, it was an event you might store for another life time.

You can see energy plays a very important role in our lives on this planet and when we're in spirit not living on the planets' surface. This energy is ageless and endless. All we have to do is continue to use it to create what we want to experience. We can make our own private holo-deck and play in it for as long as we want.

Start creating positive things in a positive way and see what you get back from the universe. Remember there are rules that even the powers of the universe have to follow. Think about what you want to create in your life. Write it down and then take the steps to manifest it into reality. This is what life is all about.

The Universe, Our Bodies and Learning

When I started my spiritual path, many ideas and thoughts came my way along with millions of questions. One idea that has stayed with me is how our bodies are like the solar system we live in. Our bodies are like individual planets that are moving and rotating here on Earth. As I learned more about energy and the energy systems we carry in our bodies, the more the universe became a metaphor for me.

It's fun to look at the human body and start relating it to the universe and all the planets. I believe we have to look at the human body as something fun or even funny. It's very complicated and many times seems to do things on its' own. Like there is a force we can't control or stop. I think we really need a sense of humor about our bodies because if I were to design a vehicle to carry my soul around in, it wouldn't be the human body. It would be something much simpler.

We're going to start this chapter with a short explanation of how our bodies work as seen in a spiritual sense combined with what science is proving. This should give you something to think about and maybe even explore on your own. Medical science is still trying to understand the body and I think that's why we call it "practicing medicine." No one really knows to this day how or why the human body does some of the things it does.

Some of the things you are going to read might seem out of this world but like any good story, there is a truth behind them. For thousands of years in many cultures there has been a belief that the human body carries with it its' own power plant, so to speak. These power centers have many books written about them and even modern medicine is starting to look into it. The power plant is made up of many different, smaller power plants that all seem to work or be connected to each other. We are going to look at the 7 main power centers and compare them to the universe and the main planets we know in our solar system.

These power centers in our bodies are known as chakras and have been recognized by spiritual groups around the world for thousands of years. We don't know everything about them, but there are several thousand books written about them and how they work. These power centers are very important to the body because they are believed to keep it balanced and working in good order if they are functioning right.

There are 7 main chakra systems in our bodies. There is also one below our feet and one just above our heads. There are at least another four or five that are above us and lead into infinity but we aren't worried about them right now. (Infinity is a human term we use to try and place a boundary on something however, infinity is as big as outer space which has no boundaries. So infinity is like saying we live forever, there is no end to it and our human brain has a problem with that concept.) Because we're living in the body, we're going to focus on the chakras that have to do with the body.

These chakras centers are energy systems that help run our lives. They are energy centers that keep us going, so to speak. It's believed that there are major benefits to learning about and having these centers run at optimal levels. That doesn't mean we want 100% of our energy running through them at a very fast rate. It means they are working together in a balanced way.

One of the benefits of learning more about the chakra system is understanding how the body, mind and spirit work together to keep the body well. Our chakras work interdependently and need each other to stay in balance, just like the planets in our universe need to be in balance for the betterment of the whole universe. Before you pooh, pooh the chakras and what they can do for you, remember medical science is proving toxins and other impurities in our food, poor environmental factors and even negative thoughts influence and trigger chemical reactions in our bodies.

As I'm writing this theory of how each chakra works together like the planets in our universe, try to compare that to how humans relate to each other. Everything in this universe is dependent on something yet we humans put our emphasis on independence instead of interdependence and working together for harmony and balance. This is where I think we are literally "missing the boat" but I don't want to get up on my soapbox about that subject so we'll just look into the chakra system.

I'm going to explain where each of the main 7 chakras are located in our bodies and what their main purpose is supposed to be in a very short and simple way. This should help you get a general idea of how they work for or against us when they're out of balance. I hope it will peak your interest into researching the chakras and becoming more aware of your own energy system and how it works. So if you're ready let's take a quick look at our chakras, what they do and how they could be related to the planets in our solar system.

Our first chakra is known as the root chakra and is located very low in the pelvic area on both men and women. This first chakra has to do with survival and grounding. Grounding our body is what makes it feel safe and in the right place at the right time. Grounding brings our soul back into the body and helps to see all the human "stuff" we are experiencing.

This first chakra is also our flight or fight system. If we are scared or angry, this center is usually working overtime and can get us into a lot of physical trouble. It really controls most of the physical things we see, experience and feel. It's very important to be aware of how much energy you're running through this system. Too much energy can make you angry all the time or give you enough fear you just want to run away from everything.

If we close this system and only have 10% of our energy running thru it, we'll feel better about a lot of things.

The second chakra is located just below your navel. Its function is desire, sexuality, pleasure and procreation. It has everything to do with the physical just like our first chakra. Some say it's where our biological clock is located because it has to do with sex and survival.

I like to use the following example of how this chakra works. In the movies when you see a man and woman in a fearful or even life threatening situation, this chakra comes into play. Usually the couple will look at each other, grab onto each other and then want to make love. All the while, you're sitting on the edge of your seat yelling, "Get out of there! Make love later! You're going to die!"

The person that wrote the movie probably didn't even understand why he wrote this scene into the movie but his body knew why. You see, when we're in a fearful situation, our first and second chakras open up to allow more energy to flow through them. If we allow all this energy to flow, we create fear. This fear creates the thought of dying but also the thought of surviving. We think we need to make love to save ourselves and the human species. What better way to ensure the continuation of man than to make love before you die?

Of course there is one thing wrong with this way of thinking; you and your partner are probably going to die so it doesn't matter if the woman gets pregnant or not because she'll soon be dead. But our energy system and DNA tells us to make love and hope for the best.

If we slowed down the flow of energy to these two chakras in any survival or panic situation, we'd realize the best thing to do is to run and make love later. These two lower chakras can run, rule and ruin our lives if we let them. Because they have everything to do with the physical world around us, we hold a lot of fear in them too. This is usually survival fear that relates to fight or flight but it can also be the fear of not having enough of something. It can bring in jealousy and competition. So we really need to control the amount of energy we are running through these two chakras.

How do we do that? By just thinking them closed more than open. Remember we are energy beings and can do anything with our thoughts. Even through these centers are in a physical human body, they are still energy centers. These two centers are very connected to each other and if one is open too much there's a good chance the other one is too.

If we can control these two chakras, we start to feel safer in our world. We can let go of anger and see the physical world as an illusion. We can understand and control our emotions more. We will be in a better place to live a better life. These two chakras are very important in understand the human way of living.

The next chakra is located just above your navel and below your breast bone. It's known as the third chakra and is the beginning of the spiritual chakras. This chakra is known as your power center. It has everything to do with how you run your emotional life.

This center has to do with how you use your power to control yourself and other people or situations. It can make us a great leader or a selfish leader. It can give us strength or if we give it to others, it can make us weak.

Let's look at a few examples to help you understand. Let's say you are a "giver". You help everyone any time they ask you. You're running to the store for them or cleaning up a mess or helping them with a choice in their life that somehow needs fixing or you're making excuses or lying for them about something or loaning them money when they could be out working.

When you're thinking with your third chakra instead of your head, you want to help everyone. That's great but everyone has to learn how to help themselves. People will never learn how to "fix" their mistakes if someone else is always doing it for them. They may also never learn how to make their own choices about life either. If you're a "fixer", there's a good possibility you're an enabler too. An enabler looks like they are doing something good for someone, but in reality, they are only helping a person NOT face responsibility for their actions and their own life.

So before you "fix" something for someone think about this. What if our actions make life worse for them? Think about it. You know they're going to blame us! Even if our intention was good, if it turned out badly it's going to be our fault. However, there is a great lesson here. The lesson is stop trying to "fix" it and let the other person figure it out for themselves. Let them change their way of doing their life because until they do, nothing can change for them.

This center can also make us a victim. If we're a victim, we blame someone, something or an experience for making us suffer for years and years. Get over it and take your power back through this third energy center. Start making your life what you want it to be. That's using this center for what it supposed to be used for – you and your power in the world.

If you find you also want to help someone, the best thing you can do is to listen to them and then ask them the most important question in the world, "What are YOU going to do about it?"

If we open up this energy center and do so much for everyone else, we will be tired and won't have the energy to do for ourselves. Our personal power center is our personal strength and should never be used for anything else or just given to someone else. Besides, if you give your personal power to someone, it will never work for them because they aren't the same vibration as you. It will never be a "fit" for them.

Another example of giving our power away is an abusive relationship. If you let someone talk to you in a degrading way or let someone physically harm you, you are giving them your power. You aren't standing up for yourself. You're letting them violate you on some level and that's taking your power from you.

So as you can see, this chakra center is very important to keep in check to maintain your personal power and integrity. This chakra is all about our personal power, emotions, intention and how to better utilize our intuitions.

The next energy center is located just above the breast bone and just below the throat area. This is the fourth chakra and has to do with how you feel about yourself and the world. It's all about your love of self and others. It has to do with love and compassion how you feel about the world in general.

If you have this chakra open too much, you'll find yourself trusting everyone and being taken for granted and used. This is not only the center that tells us how much we love ourselves but how much we should love everyone else. The problem here is if we don't love ourselves, we really can't love anyone else. When that happens, we try to love as many people as we can because something's missing. What's missing is loving yourself.

Here again, it's okay to help and love but there's a balance. If we love someone so much we think we can't live without them, that's not balance. Always remember, you lived without them before you meant them and did okay.

This fourth chakra is really about the two main emotions in this universe, love and fear. All other emotions stem from these two basic feelings. If you live with a lot of fear, you probably find you're jealous, distrustful, angry and resentful. If you live with a lot of self love, you see everything in a different prospective. You see people how they really are and you let them be what they think they need to be, even if you don't agree with it.

Love doesn't mean you have to have a sexual relationship or even a friendship. Love means you see another person as the spiritual being they are and know they're going through what they must to learn and grow. Love from this center is many different things but mostly it means you feel good about yourself and how you're living your life.

The next center is number five. It's located from the neck up to just under your nose. This chakra has to be with all our communication skills. It's not only vocal communication but body language, thoughts and other ways to communicate.

If this center is open too much, we can talk someone to death about things they don't care about. We can even talk about things we know nothing about. This center is how we communicate with the physical world as well as the spirit world. Many people think we listen with our "third eye" but we really listen to everything through this communication chakra.

The next chakra is the sixth chakra. It's located from the nose up to the top of the forehead. This is commonly known as our third eye. This is where our psychic channels are located, around the eyes. This chakra can help you "see" other dimensions and open your senses to the energy world around us. This chakra can also analyze all your thoughts. If we analyze too much, we lose our spiritual connection. Sometimes we just have to take things as they are and be okay with that.

We should monitor the flow of energy thru this chakra as too little will not allow messages in and too much can result in "thinking" too much. We also need to be careful because if you open this chakra to everything, dark entities may try to come thru.

This is where we get pictures and messages from the universe, God, angels, spirit guides or just telepathic messages from other humans here on Earth. If this center is shut down too much, we block all this communication and our own intuition. If this center is open too far, we get too much information from many different sources and it can become confusing.

If you start hearing too many voices in your head or voices that tell you to hurt someone or yourself, it's time to look at this chakra. If it's open only 70%, you will get messages but it's a reasonable amount of energy for your body to handle. Remember, because you are a energy being and your chakras are energy centers, it can all be controlled with your thoughts, because thoughts are energy.

It's as simple as thinking your energy systems open or closed. It may take some practice to feel them or "know" when they are working right, but with time and being conscious of them, you'll learn to control them.

The next chakra is located just above your head and is the seventh chakra. This energy system is where the Light from the universe comes into your body. It's also where we open up to the whole spiritual side of our world.

If this center is open too much, we may feel lightheaded and ungrounded. We might not be able to make decisions because we feel like we're in a different world. Having this energy center open too much invites all kinds of trouble and other beings who are in spirit. This is where we channel others and if we allow them access, they can jump in and take over.

When you are working with any of your energy centers, caution is advised until you learn how they work and how to control them. Opening and closing them in an unhealthy way can affect your health and well-being. It's important to get all the information you can on these centers before you start any activity with them.

So these are the seven main energy systems in your body. We also have an energy centers under our feet, in the palms of our hands and in almost every joint in our bodies. There may also be as many as 5 more energy centers above our heads. These centers help us connect to the heavens but because at this time we really aren't sure about them and what they do, we won't worry about them. When the time is right, they will start to come into our reality and maybe we'll even discover other planets beyond Pluto that has some connection to them.

As I've pointed out, the first two chakras have everything to do with the physical world of matter , sex and fight or flight. The five above your navel have everything to do with the spiritual side of things. These are the chakras we should pay the most attention too so we can keep ourselves safe. They help us see and really understand what life is all about.

If we keep the energy flow of the first two chakras closed down to only 10% or 20%, we keep them under control. We can view the physical world from a healthy stand point instead of viewing it with fear or anger. If we keep the other five chakras open and energy running through them at about 70%, we'll have a great prospective on the spiritual world and how it works. We'll start to manifest our lives in the way we want. We'll see life is a learning experience and we can make up some of the rules as we go.

So what does all this have to do with our universe? Well this universe is pretty much run by the number 7, as I've pointed out earlier. We have seven days in a week. We have seven chakras. There are seven major planets not including Earth. Because Pluto has been reclassified as a non-planet because of it's size we can't count it here; however we are going to use it in this example because I think it's important in the whole realm of the universe.

So let's take our seven main chakras and compare them to our universe and the planets. Let's just say the sun is our higher power. The power that created us and supplies life to us. (Remember this is just so you can see that everything is connected and has some meaning in this universe. I'm not saying the sun is God or anything else.)

In this metaphoric example, we have a higher power that doesn't seem to move. It's there as solid as a rock, so to speak. It comes up every day and sets every night. We take it for granted. We just expect it will keep coming up and setting every day, every night, and every decade until it burns out in about 5 billion years. We really never think about it and what it does for us.

We don't usually think about the other planets and what they do for us either. Without them, we wouldn't be here. They help keep us in balance and keep our place in the universe. They are in the heavens to keep the balance. If one of them is out of aliment, the universe goes out of aliment.

I don't know what would happen but I think our universe would collapse and everything fall apart if something was out of aliment with the planets. This is what happens to us when our chakra system is out of aliment. If we are running too much energy through one chakra and not enough through another, we can get out of aliment as well.

When our chakra system is out of balance, our whole system is out of balance. An example is if we are thinking of sex all the time, we can't get clear message from our soul because we are obsessed with the physical things in life. This could bring in feelings of jealously or feeling unimportant to someone. It can bring in all kinds of negative emotions and then we can and usually do make fools of ourselves.

The planets are metaphors for our chakras and the stars are metaphors for how many souls there are in our universe; at least let's look at it that way just for fun.

Let's look at Earth as our body and see where the planets are in comparison to us. Two of the smallest planets, Mercury and Venus, are located next to the sun and are the first and second planets. This could be our first and second chakras. There is also a reason these two planets are small and closer I'm sure. I feel it's because their gravitational pull on us is less than the larger planets and therefore it helps keep the Earth where it should be in the universe. Their gravitational pull is not as strong so even when they are in their closest orbit to us, there is no threat.

These two planets are metaphors for our first and second chakras so we need to look at their size as a metaphor too. In other words, these two chakras should have less energy moving around and through them to help us stay safe and balanced. Because our first two chakras have everything to do with the body and all our physical reality, these two planets are closer so we can see them and explore them. They represent our need to see and touch something so we believe it's real.

These planets are close enough that we can visually see them and you know how visual us humans are. Visualization is a big part of dealing with the physical. We know that many of the other planets are so far away we can't really see them so we don't give them much thought.

Mercury is a small planet, just a little bigger than Pluto. So if it represents our first chakra, our fight or flight center, we should take a lesson from it. It's really saying that our fears about life should be the smallest thing we are focusing on.

I think this planet is a great metaphor for many things in our physical world. It represents why our body is here. It's call the root chakra because it really does make our body feel rooted to the Earth. It's also very close to the next planet, Venus, which would represent our sexuality so I would imagine these two planets work together just like the first two chakras of our bodies.

Mercury is also the closest planet to the sun which makes it very hot. Is this a metaphor for our sexual actions or even the Kundalini energy that runs through our body?

Kundalini is a psycho-spiritual energy that is thought to reside in a sleeping body but comes to life either through spiritual discipline or spontaneous actions which bring about new states of consciousness. The kundalini energy is described as liquid fire and liquid light and when you feel it in your life, you'll never forget it. With a description like that, it could be talking about Mercury and the heat it possesses.

The second planet is Venus, which we think of as a female goddess. This is interesting because the next planet is Earth and then Mars as a male god. We are positioned between the masculine and feminine energies of the universe. How fun is that! So we have a planet that represents our sexuality followed by the two planets we think of as representing our sexes.

Venus is the second planet and would represent some of our sexual feelings along with some flight or fight feelings too. Remember, our energy centers have to work together to work right just like the planets in the heavens have to work together to keep the Universe balanced.

Venus represents the feminine. We could say it is the planet that holds our sexual and creative emotions. This is the energy we use before we go forward with actions. That's what the feminine energy does. Maybe this is why the flight or fight emotions are so strong and we stop to think about which one we want to do before we do it, well most of the time.

Also think about how we view people when we think about Mars and Venus. Men are from Mars, the God, and women are from Venus, the Goddess. Maybe we know more than we think we do about this universe and the planets.

Who would have thought a book would have been written about it? However this comparison has been going on for thousands and thousands of years throughout many different cultures. What started us thinking we might be from another planet or even that the planets had something to do with us? Have we known all along we are attached more to outer space then to Earth? Is that why we are so drawn to the sky, the stars and the planets?

Mars would represent our third chakra which would be our power center. This represents how we use our personal power. This would run right along with the masculine energy of control. Control can be a good thing or an overbearing thing. This is the masculine energy but it has to work with the feminine energy of Venus to get anything done.

If you look at all the planets we have just mentioned, they are close together and rotate close to help each other. So we see how the first, second and third chakras can work together to help us make wise choices.

If we don't give all our power to our sexuality, we can think about whether we are going to stay in a situation or leave it, this is fight or flight. Then we can use our personal power to become stronger in any situation. This is how our chakras work together and how the planets work together. Our chakra systems rotate and spin and so do the planets. Movement and balance runs this Universe from our bodies to the outer limits of our galaxy.

The next planet is Jupiter. A good example of how the universe works for us is Jupiter. Jupiter is the largest planet and is placed in the Universe as a shield to Earth. Because of the gravitational pull of this planet, many meteorites that would fly into Earth are diverted.

This happens when meteorites that are headed our way fly close enough for the gravitational pull of this large planet to either pull them into the planets' surface and be burnt up or the gravitational force grabs the objects and flings it around the planet in a sling-shot way and throws it back into outer space. Now who thought of that? What a wonderful shield for us here on Earth.

It's also interesting that Jupiter would be our fourth chakra, how we feel about ourselves and others, both spiritually and emotionally. Are we safe? How do we like ourselves? How do we view the world?

In other words, it's a shield against the rocks people can throw at us in our world. It helps shield us from hurt feelings. This what Jupiter's does for Earth. It's the unseen power that helps keep us safe. It shields us and gives a sense of safety from anything that might come flying our way.

That's what our fourth chakra can do for us. It can make us see everything that comes our way can either be taken in or throw aside because we don't need it.

It's also the biggest planet in the solar system, which can equate to "a big heart". However, when you have a big heart, you have to have a powerful force behind it to keep it safe. The power of this planet would be it's gravitational pull. In our bodies this pull would be the pull we feel when we love someone or something. We feel drawn to it and want to be close to it.

This is what this planet does too. It either brings the meteors to it's surface or throws them back into space. We do the same thing in our lives. When we love something, we bring it close but when we are done with it, we throw it away or get rid of it.

This planet also has a gaseous surface where nothing can survive. Does this sound like heartburn? Does this planet represent our heart and love as well as our stomach? And if it does, is that why we are so obsessed with food? This is the biggest planet in our system. Does it represent the over abundance of food we have and our waist lines?

There is a lot to think about when we think about Jupiter. It would represent our love, pain, shielding our emotions and feelings and everything we "take to heart".

The next planet would be Saturn, our fifth chakra. This is our communication center. It's the second biggest planet which should tell us that communication might be one of our priorities. So if you put the two biggest planets together, Jupiter and Saturn, and what they represent, it's love and communication.

Are these the two biggest lessons we are here to learn? As humans do we really do this well? Not really.

We think love is sex and communication is telling someone what we want them to do. You'd think as old as we are we would have learned these lessons by now but maybe that's just part of being human. What I find interesting is the first three planets are very close to Earth but as we move onto the other planets, they get farther apart from each other.

Mercury, Venus and Mars are very close but Jupiter is almost 4 times farther away from it's closest neighbor. Does the distance between the planets also represent the space we have to close between our spiritual soul and our physical body. As the planets get farther away from Earth and from each other, are they representing the distance in energy we need to close to become one with ourselves?

As we look at Saturn, we see there are rings around it. What would these rings represent in our physical world? Do they represent the energy around our bodies we call an aura? After all, our aura is around our body like a ring.

Is this ring of energy that surrounds our body part of our communication system? Is our communication center more than just speaking, writing, body language and other physical ways we communicate with each other? Do the rings represent the unseen physical and spiritual communication we have?

We aren't sure why Saturn has these rings but if we relate them to us, I feel they do represent the energy fields around our bodies. Our aura is that unseen energy you can feel, therefore it has to be part of how we communicate.

I believe the auras around our bodies are part of our communication system. It's energy we put out that tells others how we are feeling even if they can't see it, they can feel it. This aura is around everything on Earth because it's energy. There's even one around Earth.

Our auras are atoms and protons and other energy charged particles that change with the energy from each different thought we think. It's a silent communication that's built in and something we don't think about.

An aura is the energy we feel when we walk into a room full of people and instantly know if you like someone or not. It's that feeling you have of "I don't know why I like them, I just do" sense about someone. An aura is an incredible energy that can help us heal or make us sick.

This is part of the human body. It's around our bodies like the rings of Saturn. We can see the rings of gases around Saturn but is that only because as humans we need that visual to relate it to our aura?

The next planet is Uranus. This would be our sixth chakra and considered our third eye. What do we know about this planet? Not very much. This is what we know about our third eye or psychic abilities. We don't understand it and it seems we really don't care. I mean, how many times have you heard someone in the space program saying, "Let's go explore Uranus."?

It's like someone saying to you, "let's explore your psychic side." What would your reaction be? Uranus may not be the biggest planet in our system but I feel once we get to know more about it, we'll find it's probably very powerful in a way we have yet to discover. It's also 4 times larger than Earth.

Does that mean our psychic side is 4 times greater than our whole body? Does that mean we should be using this energy more than the energy of our first chakra? I think that's something we need to think about.

The next planet would be Neptune. This would be our seven chakra or the chakra known as the crown chakra. This chakra isn't in our body but sits just outside on the top of our heads.

It represents the energy center where we receive Light and messages from the universe.

It's also 4 times larger than Earth. I think it's interesting that the two planets representing our two most psychic chakras are both 4 times larger than Earth. There has to be some meaning to that.

The last planet would be Pluto which is not considered a planet anymore because of its size. However, it does represent another chakra that connects us to the outer limits of the spiritual world and energy. This would be one of the new chakras we are just starting to learn about; which is what is happening with Pluto.

We first thought of Pluto as a planet but now the scientists are saying it's too small to be considered a planet. It might be small but it's one of the most mysterious planets we have in the universe so far. We don't know a lot about this planet and we don't know a lot about the other chakras above our heads that go out into space and the unseen spirit world. Some day we'll know more about both.

What we do know about Pluto is this. Pluto's orbit is different from other planets. Pluto is the most highly inclined and elliptical of the all planets. This actually brings Pluto closer to the sun than Neptune for part of its' orbit. The axis rotation for most planets are nearly perpendicular to the ecliptic but Uranus and Pluto are exceptions. They are tipped on their sides. I find it fascinating that these two planets, one representing our third eye and one representing communication from a higher power, rotate differently from the rest of the planets. Is that we do in our body too?

Another thing I find interesting is the size and what we know about the planets. The planets that represent most of the "Earthly" emotions or tangible objects are the smallest planets and the ones we know the most about. The planets that represent more spiritual thoughts and feelings are the larger planets and still need to be explored in many different ways. If we learn by example, maybe we should study this theory more before we think we're ready to move on.

We're already proving there are thousands of other galaxies known to us. We are just now finding out that our galaxy is traveling through intergalactic space just like all the other galaxies. No galaxy is standing still. They are all moving through space. How big does that make space? I don't think our human brain can even comprehend that!

Thinking about how we are actually moving through space and knowing that other galaxies are doing the same thing brings up more questions. Are aliens visiting us or are we traveling through their front yards as our systems moves through the cosmos? And if we are moving through space, what comes next?

What we need to learn is everything is or has energy and is in consist movement of some kind. This movement is the change we need for creation of different experiences. That's how everything is created, even in other solar systems, it has to be. There has to be movement to create something.

Is this why humans are always on the move? Movement creates energy that creates changes that creates new realities or experiences. Movement means change. Change means creating. Creating relieves boredom and stress. With this in mind, is this system so different from any other system?

Could the other systems be somewhat like this one? Of course! Only here we're human and who knows what life form we are in other galaxies. I'm sure we need to be in life forms that best suits other galaxies and the lessons we are supposed to learn there.

This might be the only system where we have all these chakras so we can learn more about energy. As we get to know more about the planets in our system, maybe we'll start to understand our own energy systems better? Maybe all beings in all other galaxies are going through something similar. I don't even pretend to know the answer to that question.

The next solar system we go into might be totally different. There might just be stars and only one planet – who knows. All we know, and really care about, is this system because it's the one we'll living in now.

In this solar system, the sun composes over 90% of it. The planets are another .135%; the comets are .01% and so on. So the sun is really the most important part of the universe. If we look at it as our creator, we see it gives us life. Without the sun we couldn't survive on this planet or any other. So it's a good thing it's as big as it is. It is the source of everything on this planet. If we relate that to a greater power who made this universe and us, we can see just how small we are in the larger picture.

However, even though we may be only a small part of the picture, without us the picture isn't complete. The power that made everything views each one of us as a very important part of the whole. Just like we view every small part of our body as important.

Each of us are individual Earths and without us, there wouldn't be a complete solar system. What would be missing? We would be missing and the individual way we create life. There would be a void and there really are no voids.

Our solar system may appear to have an empty void between planets and stars but just like the space between our inner organs, it's full of various forms of energy. There is all kinds of interplanetary dust and solid particles of matter we aren't sure about.

This is also like our bodies. We really don't understand the human form yet; after all we have only been human for a very short time. We still have thousands and millions of years to go before we'll really understand the human body. I think in the next million years or so, we'll mutate into another form that will be like a human but better.

I'm sure as we study the universe and our own energy system, we'll find more and more similarities. However you can start right now by looking into your energy system and becoming more and more familiar with your own body.

Getting to know your body, how it functions, what it likes and dislikes and what keeps it healthy is very important. Learning about the physical body, the aura around your body and your energy body, will help you understand how this world works

Everything that is born or created in this Universe lives, fulfills its purpose and dies.

Because our soul isn't from this Universe, it doesn't die. Our soul is run by different laws because it was created long before this Universe was even formed. Things not of this Universe are not governed by the rules of this Universe.

Once something is born or created on Earth, it is part of Earth. Our bodies have many of the main elements and minerals that make up Earth. We are mostly water and so is the Earth. We have copper, lead, zinc and other elements so our body can go back into the Earth when we are finished here.

Our soul is pure energy and not from this Earth. It's from outer space, far beyond our own galaxy. Our soul doesn't have to play by the same rules our bodies do so therefore it's free to do what it wants.

As I'm finishing this chapter, I'm on a flight from Salt Lake City to Phoenix Arizona. My dad has suddenly become very ill. He's in the hospital and it seems he only has a few days to live. As of an hour ago, his blood pressure was 82/43. I told him telepathically to hang on if he could until I get there to say good bye. I find it strangely comforting he's starting his transition to the other side as I'm writing a book about how old our souls and the life we continue with after we leave this Earthly plane.

I'm sure his crossing is helping me channel much of the information I've just written. I feel his physical and energy bodies are both tired and soon he'll be home resting. Even as I check into his system from high in the air, I can feel his chakras moving slowly, like wheels grinding to a halt. His life force is tired and he's leaking energy like a tire with a nail in it.

The body is an amazing invention but it's not perfect. The only thing that's perfect is our soul. I hope he can hang on until I get there, but if he can't I'll tell him now, "Good bye Daddy, I love you! Go back home and rest. Go into outer space and explore – watch over me and help guide me with the wisdom you have from this lifetime and from the spirit world that you'll soon be part of – home is a good place to be."

Why Don't We Remember

There are several theories about why we don't remember being on Earth over and over again. There's also one very good reason why things seem new to us all the time even though we are billions of years old. That reason is each life is a new one.

We don't remember a lot of our past lives because, as stated earlier, the trauma of birth and death makes us forget. Also, if we remembered everything, there would be no reason to come back. Could you imagine everyone on Earth knowing exactly why they came here? How boring!

If everyone remembered their past lives, the ego would really get in the way of learning. Say you were a king or very wealthy in your past life and remembered it. You might expect to be treated like royalty in this life time and you aren't.

This would make you a very hard person to deal with because no one but you remembers you were a king in that life. In this life you might be a homeless person just so you can learn what it's like to be without the material things you had in your last life.

We really only need to remember the lessons we learned in our past lives so they will help us in the present life. Our energy body will bring forward lessons we have already learned to help us with this life and to let us know we don't have to go through that lesson again, unless we want too. Some of us choose to go through the same lessons over and over again. I'm not sure why we do this, but I think we might be hoping the outcome will be different.

There's a saying, "If you do something the someway all the time, you'll get the same results." So if you are doing something in your life and it's not going well or coming out the way you want it too, stop doing it. You are either not supposed to do it or you are supposed to do it a different way.

When we come back to Earth, we don't usually go through the same lessons unless we have committed suicide and didn't get as far with our life as we were supposed too. Once we learn a lesson, we move on. The same lesson might present its self to us in a number of different ways but when we get to the point of seeing it and knowing what it is in all forms, it stops coming to us. We can then move on to a different lesson.

Most of us are learning several lessons at the same time. That's what makes life so interesting. So if we get the lessons, why come back? Because each time we come back, we are in a different time and place and there are different things to learn in each of these places and that will change the lesson every time.

Just imagine for a minute how many places there are on Earth. How many different countries, cities, mountains, deserts, oceans and all the other places you could go. You can't visit all of them in one life time.

Each town has different ideas and problems to solve just like each country, continent and hemisphere. Each area of this world is different even if these areas are only a few miles apart. There are different belief systems in all these areas. How could we visit and learn all of this in one life time? We can't.

Also each time we come back, it's a different time so everything is different and new. Today is different from tomorrow and last year is different from this year. If things didn't change, we would be coming back to the same place and the same time period.

Even in this life time, everyday is different and new. When we wake up in the morning, it's a different time in time. That sounds funny but tomorrow isn't today. It's one day later than yesterday. Time keeps moving no matter what we do. Everyday has it's own new experiences and adventures as well as opportunities to change the way we do things.

If we didn't move through time, everything would be the same everyday. Nothing would change. Remember the movie "Groundhog Day". It would be like that.

An example would be coming back to the middle ages, to the same town, with the same parents, the same brothers or sisters and living the same life over again and again. How boring would that be? There'd be no real reason for living, would there?

But with the constant changing of things here on Earth, the other planets in our solar system, time and everything else, we can experience different things every time we come back. That's why every thing seems different to us every time we're here – because they really are!

The only things that stay the same are feelings and emotions. Fear is the same as it was two thousand years ago. There maybe different fears but fear is still fear. We may not fear being hung as a witch or being thrown into an arena to be eaten by lions, but we still have many basic fears. We fear dying, we fear living, we fear losing something, we fear getting something, we fear nothing will go right and we fear nothing will go wrong. Man, with all this fear no wonder humans are so screwed up.

I heard something the other day and I thought how true it was and I'd like to share it with you. A Native American chief was asked where he thought the white man went wrong. (And I'm sure we could trace something like this back to every land on this Earth at one time or another, but I'm just using this as an example.)

The chief was old and had lived when the natives were the only people on this land. He had seen the white man come and what they had done to devastate the land and animals. He thought for a moment and then said, "When white man find land, Indians running it, no taxes, no debt, plenty buffalo, plenty beaver, clean water. Women did all the work, Medicine man was free. Indian man spend all day hunting and fishing; all night having sex." Then he smiled and added, "Only white man dumb enough to think he could improve system like that."

So goes the way of advancement, invention and whatever else you need to label it. It's progress and change. No one's saying it's wrong or right, it just is. We have to keep creating things, good or bad. It's what we do. It's who we are. It's a given because whatever created us is still creating and we are proving it with our technology today.

Science is proving everything in this world and in the outer space world is made up of atoms, molecules and other living organisms that only a few of us understand. They're proving our bodies are made up of small energy systems too. These are the chakras we talked about earlier. They are also proven our joints have energy around them.

Our bodies are a mass of tiny moving parts that somehow come together and stay together to form a semi-solid entity we call a human being. All these parts work together and do what they have to do to keep the body alive. We never think about it until something goes wrong.

We don't think about our heart beating until it jumps a beat or stops. We don't think about some of our skin washing off every morning in the shower. We don't think about anything until it's brought to our attention and then many times it's too late. Doesn't that make the best argument for us coming back time after time after time? And even the phase I just used is a good one to think about? Time after time after time – that's all we have.

We'll never run out of time because it's a promise – we live forever. There is no time in forever. There just is. Everything just is right now. That's why we keep coming back and learning new things; because literally everything we come back to is new, except emotions.

Fear and love never change. There are hundreds and thousands of emotions that come from these two feelings but they really never change. Is that why we come back?

We only know love on the other side and it's a different love than we look for here.

The love on the other side is one of knowing everything is okay all the time. It's not being judged or wanting for anything. It's a love so great I can't explain it. I've felt it because I was there once but you can't explain it because it doesn't exist on this side. There is no human love that feels like the love on the other side. It's better than hot cocoa on a snowy day. It's better than Christmas morning and a million presents. It's better than the best of any thing you've ever experienced.

It's not a feeling in your heart because you don't have a heart when you're in spirit. It's just a feeling all around you of comfort, joy, happiness and well being. There are no words to describe it. There is no feeling like it on this side.

Here on Earth we have so much we can do, create and live! I don't think we could get bored ever because every time we come back, it's a new time and things have changed. I know people who hate change. They gripe about it all the time, but how boring would it be to do the same thing every day. Of course I have to add right here that many of us do just that; the same thing every day.

We get up at the same time, we take our shower at the same time, we go to work at the same time, we eat our meals at the same time and maybe we even have the same food all the time.

I once knew a man who ate a boloney and cheese sandwich every night for dinner. Seriously, he did this for years. He hated veggies and when he died of a heart attack, the new wrapping that comes on a stove and oven was still on it. The oven was 5 years old and he had never cooked anything on it. I think he missed out on one of the greatest adventures we have on this side, FOOD!

I think that might be another reason we come back. We made the human body so we could taste, see, hear, feel, smell, touch and enjoy all those physical things here on Earth. That's what Earth is all about – the physical side of us.

I know we do some of these things on the other side, but we don't have taste buds. Out of all the senses, this is the one I would like to be able to take with us. The people on the other side show me the food they eat, but it's different from eating it here. It's energy. It's like eating something without the real taste. It's rather boring and that's why spirits don't eat, they just bring energy to themselves and use it like we use food for our body's' energy.

On the other side food is like looking at a picture of fried chicken and then eating the picture not the actual chicken. When we're on the other side we can see, hear, smell, feel and in some way touch but we really can't taste.

Is that why food is such a big deal here? Guess that's more "food for thought". All of us are obsessed with food. We either eat too much or not enough. We have "fast food", home-cooked food, Chinese, Japanese, Mexican, Greek, American and all kinds of different foods from different places around the world. We even have junk food. And why do we call it junk food, because if you really look at it, it's not the best stuff to be stuffing into your mouth.

Maybe we eat really healthy or maybe we don't. We're always trying to find the balance between these two. No matter what we do, food is at the top of our list all the time. We can't seem to understand it or even agree on what is the best for us but we all agree it tastes great. Food is very much a part of any life here on Earth, from the smallest bug to the largest plant and animal. Everything on Earth "eats" in one way or another.

When we have holidays or family "get togethers" we have food. When friends come over, we have food. When we are talking on the phone, we eat. When we are lonely, happy, sad, and mad or many other emotions, we eat. Sports mean snacking foods. There's romantic dinners for two; movies with popcorn and candy; weddings, funerals, wakes, births, and so much more. All these things are important parts of our lives.

There are very few people who can go with out eating but there are a few. These people are called breatharians. A breatharian is a person who is nourished by light and seems to have no need for food or drink. It is thought by some that people who feel drawn to living on light nourishment can activate their body to do without food, but this is not an easy task. There are several books about breatharians and their diets. I personally don't know any breatharians but I keep an open mind to everything. After all, I don't think the Lemurians needed food either.

Each life time is a different time, a different place, there's different food, different people, a different body to get used too and all the other tens of thousands of things that are different. So when we come back to Earth, we are like new little beings even though we are billions of years old and have been back to Earth hundreds or maybe thousands of times.

Each time is different and that's all part of the master plan. I think the biggest part of the master plan is to live, create and learn. Each time we're here, we take back information and experiences to share with other souls. Earth's a place of great learning.

However our human brains only remember the "stuff" we learn in the body we are presently in. We don't bring back the same brain with us each time. It's always a different brain, but we always have the same energy body or soul. That never changes. I feel it's our energy body that remembers everything. I also feel the energy body can't down load all the information it stores into the human brain all at once.

Maybe that's why we only use a tenth of our brain. Maybe the rest of our gray matter is just used for storage. The energy of these memories are so great, it can't be downloaded all at once because it would be too much for the human brain tissue. It might just explode our brains. It might be like trying to download all the information you have stored on five computers onto one at the same time. It just might be too much information for us to handle at any one time.

We can say we are all old souls but with each life we're new because we have a new body. The Universe is expanding and changing every second of every day. Even the Earth is changing all the time. The animals are changing too. Many die out because they are no longer needed or fit well with the changes on Earth. Some evolve into something else better equipped for the future of Earth. There are patterns but even the patterns change.

This is why we keep coming back; because it's an adventure every time. Humans have adventure in their blood. It's like it's part of our DNA and maybe it is because who made us certainly had adventure in their DNA. Just trying to create a human out of dirt had to have it moments.

Adventure is also change. Whether we want to admit it or not, change is healthy. Even the change of getting old and dying is a healthy event. What good would it be to stay here forever and be old and miserable. Isn't it better to leave the body and return in a new one? That's a healthy change no matter what angle you look at it from.

The event of dying and coming back also allows us to process the lessons we have learned this time around. They are stored as reminders to help us the next time. So in the great realm of the continuum, we know a lot about the past but the future is still a mystery because it's an ever changing process of creation. Nothing's set in stone. Change is just a natural part of creation, evolution, learning and the wonder of life on this planet and all the planets in all the solar systems.

Being a psychic, I want to add something here about what a psychic can and can not read about you. Psychics don't know every thing because everything is changing. We're living in a time when we have more free will and choices than ever before. So if a psychic tells you something is going to happen to you on a certain day at a certain time, laugh at them. They have just taken away your free will and put a seed of doubt in your head.

Only you have the free will to change things. Here's an example; if someone tells you you'll be in an accident in a green car on Sept. 1 at 2:00 pm, don't get into a green car or any other car that day. Also if the information a psychic is giving to you doesn't feel right, don't take it to heart. Lots of things can be misinterpret between this dimension and the spirit world. Sometimes it's like trying to tell what someone is saying when they are talking under water.

Psychics, healers, counselors, hypnotherapists, and others you work with should only help you remember, not plant doubt or untruths in your mind. In most cases, all of us will remember things on our own. We have all had "déjà vu". That's just a remembrance of a past life sparked by something in this life. It can happen anywhere and at any time. In other cases we may need help in remembering but we don't need someone planting a seed of doubt in our human brain.

Our human brain is very willing to accept lies if we let our ego get in the way. Not all of us have been royalty or the Queen of Sheba and it's okay. Not all of lived in Jesus' time. Not all of us have been Vikings. So we have to be careful what others try to get us to believe. If it fits and feels good, it's probably the truth. If it doesn't, it's probably not the truth about who we were.

Because this might be the only place in space where we are human, we can't count on the human brain to remember everything. I think this is why we're so unsure about many things in our lives. We run them past our human brain instead of running them past our soul. I've decided to start the process of running emotions, thoughts and ideas past my soul before I do anything with them. I'm going to trust that my soul knows more than my human brain and see what happens.

I believe this can help me see where my own life is going and what the future holds for me. We all want to see into the future but if we lived more in the present and made wise choices here, our future would pretty much take care of its self

I know my soul can help me with emotions because emotions never really change, only the situations that bring up the same emotion changes. Every time we learn not to be jealous, another situation comes up to test us on it until the thought of jealously doesn't even come up. Then we can have a life time where jealousy isn't a factor.

This could be another reason we keep coming back. We have to get to the point where emotions mean nothing more than a healing for us. Do we need to get to a point where emotions don't control us and they don't own us? Are we here to just feel what emotions are, look at what is causing that feeling and then let it go? Is this Earth school really a fun way of saying, "Wow this is different from the other side. This is riding the roller coaster at the fair with all its ups and downs and twists and turns. It goes fast in some places and slows down in others. What a ride it is to be human!"

Not many of us look at life in that manner. Nor do we look at our emotions as fun or just another way of exercising our free will, but that's really what they are. Emotions are learning experiences in how we can use our free will to overcome them and get them out of our way so we can see what is really going on in our lives. Remember everything here on Earth seems to have a metaphoric meaning of some kind.

Emotions can be like a mosquito buzzing in your ear. At first you ignore it but after awhile it becomes an irritant and you have to do something about it. You can keep swatting at it but it just keeps coming back. Then it lands on you and tries to bite you. This is when you can't ignore it anymore and you have to eliminate it.

Emotions are like that. If we don't do something about them, we can't let them go. It's not good to ignore an emotion, it's good to feel it, examine it and then let it go. Just pushing it away won't get rid of it. You have to face it and walk through it. You have to make choices and they might be tough choices to deal with but until you deal with them, they'll be a mosquito buzzing in your ear and feeding on your blood.

This is where your soul and the knowledge it holds can help you to learn. If you feel you've been through a situation before but can't remember when, it was probably in another life. That's your soul remembering. Your soul is saying, "Hey, you've been here before. You don't have to go through this again."

It wants to help you remember you have either already learned this lesson or experienced the event and it's really not necessary to go do it again.

Once we have the knowledge of how to live with emotions but not to become them, we start a very different path. It's a path to enlightenment but more importantly it's a path to not having to keep returning to Earth to go thru emotions over and over again.

Someone asked me the other day if we ever get to the place of Nirvana, or total peace, so we can unite with the Godhead.

I said, "Of course we do. We can do that any time we want whether we're here or on the other side. We visit "God" all the time. But we are driven souls who have to keep learning and growing and so we break away and go out on our own." I think this might be where the story of the "fallen angels" came from. I don't believe any of us are fallen angels, just individuals going out on their own to learn, experience and grow.

Being with the Godhead is great but the Power we think of as "God or Goddess" is still growing and expanding. This concept is hard for many of us to believe but I don't think a power that is big enough to make this Universe and us is just going to stop here. I wouldn't! I'd be out there creating and growing and expanding and doing all kinds of cool things. This is what I believe is still happening and no matter what we "call this Power" it's still creating and growing.

We can go to the Godhead whether our body is alive or dead, we just need to ask and go. The problem lies in the belief we can't do it that easy. Our Creator made everything easy. We turned it into something hard with our belief systems. It's simple. If you live simply, you spend more time creating, living and being in touch with yourself and the Higher Power. You don't get caught up in the illusion of life and all the physical and visual items, events and emotions.

I think everything we learn and the way we live is really connected to the master plan of what life is supposed to be about. It's coming to Earth to be in a body to learn different things at different times and never fail at any of it. Wow, now there's something I can understand and really embrace. It really makes sense to me. Human life is just another way we are expressing ourselves.

Another misconception is "life" has to be in a human form to be "life". Our brain can't understand "life" is everywhere. It's in the air we breath. It's in a drop of water. It's in everything we see and everything we don't see. Even a rock is alive with moving atoms and particles if you look close enough and some of these rocks are over 100 billion years old.

So if a rock is that old, why can't our souls be at least that old? Humans have a lot of sayings and one is, "If this building could talk, it would it have a lot to say." Well, let your soul talk to you and bring forward the knowledge of your past lives. Many people don't believe in reincarnation and that's okay, it's their opinion and belief system. I believe in it because of everything I have experienced and that's my opinion too.

However I believe if you start talking to your soul, it will tell you what you already know; not from the ego but from the energy body. Let's say you somehow know you were a witch in the middle ages. You don't know why but you feel you were. You feel you did some healing or good things as a witch but your brain says, "Witches are evil".

Yet you feel like you know how to put healing herbs and other things together to help people. Even in this lifetime you are interested in healing herbs or natural remedies and just seem to know what ones go together naturally. So you start too study some facts about witches and find out you have to go back farther than the 1300's to really get the truth about them.

The word witch means "wise". Wicca means "wise one" and Witchcraft means "craft of the wise." A witch was a respected member of the community prier to 1000 AD. They helped ease pain and healed people and their animals. Witches used hypnosis to make childbirth pain free. It was the Christian movement that said these powers came from the Devil.

The Christian movement created a lot of fear among people. The people back then wanted power over the people and did this through fear. I'm not saying all aspects of the movement were bad but it really put the fear of "God' into the world and we've been trying to get rid of it ever since.

Even to this day, people "kill in the name of God" to justify murdering thousands of innocent people. They use His name to get what they want. More people have been killed in the name of some "god" than any other types of killings. I don't believe God wanted this at all. He must still be wondering what the hell happened to us when we became human.

Too much blood was shed during the holy crusades. Too much power was given to too few men. These men didn't understand witchcraft and the good it did, but the larger piece of the puzzle was they wanted to rule over the women. They wanted the power the women or witches had so they had to make witches look bad.

This was the start of the underground healing world. Everyone that wanted to go to a witch for healing had to do it very carefully and in the dark of night. That's why witches are associated with the dark. (just a side note – the pictures of witches with disfigured, green faces we use on Halloween is taken from the fact many witches were beat to death. The green represents the bruising of the face and the disfigurement is from the beating.)

Telepathy, faith healing, pre-cognition, clairvoyance and astral-travel were all part of the practice of witchcraft in the past as was the knowledge of plants and healing herbs. But during and after the witch hunts and trials, no one wanted to risk their life by going to a witch for healing. People went to a priest who took their money, made them fearful of God and told them what to believe in. This time period was ripe with fear and many people were afraid if they didn't believe in God and the church, they would be damned to hell. All the church clergy told them this was the way it was. There was a story spread that said if you didn't have enough faith in God, you would get sick and die.

Pretty stupid stuff but it's still believed today. Many so called holy men where the worst of the worst back in these dark days. They killed, robbed, raped and beat anyone who got in their way. It was a terrible time for humans because it seemed their free will had been taken away and all the magic of life was sucked dry by some very evil forces.

There had been a time when magicians and seers were priests and priests were magicians and seers. Then greed and power got in the way and even the priests forgot about the magic they could do. It's too bad because I think if the priests were still magicians maybe more people would go to church now.

But I regress, we were talking about you starting to remember you had been a witch at one time or another in your past. As you research witches, you "seem to know" about healing herbs and other things only witches might have known about. The research you are doing about witches seems more like you're reading about something you have already experienced.

The more you read about witches, the more you start to feel like you have done this work before or maybe you feel like you were burned at the stake. You could have all kinds of feelings in your body or just a knowing in your brain. This is part of your energy body telling you there is stored knowledge about a past life in your system. All you have to do is start remembering.

Many people call it "imagination". Imagination meant "image in energy" in ancient times. This is what our energy body does. It stores energy images that we can access when we need them. This also means when we see a shadowy figure out of the corner of our eye, it's an image in energy. We couldn't imagine it if it didn't exist in some form.

If you are talking to someone about a past event in history and they feel strongly about it but you feel nothing, you probably weren't alive at that time in history. Not all of us have been in a human body in every century or even every millennium. When we move from this world of energy to the spirit world of energy, we may have to rest and regenerate our energy body. As I've stated before, being human is hard on our energy bodies and that's why we are looked at as heroes by the angels.

Once we start remembering things from our soul, things just seem to come to us. This is our energy body telling us what we've been through before. If we start listening to it, life becomes so much clearer.

However, because energy is always moving and flowing, sometimes we have to find the right spot in the flow or time to be able to bring this knowledge forward.

Because we don't remember that our energy body has stored all this information, it may take a couple of different experiences about the same subject for us to remember.

It's like the old records we used to play before CD's. Each song was recorded on it and you could pick up the record players' arm and put it down on a certain song you wanted to hear. (For those of you that have never seen a record player, it was like pushing the play button on your CD player to find the right track that has your favorite song on it.) Boy I think I'm dating myself here.

Anyway, this is the way we remember lessons and lives from the past. Usually remembering a life from the past isn't that important unless it has something to do with your life in the present.

Here are a couple of examples.

I could never seem to wear a turtleneck sweater and feel comfortable in it. No matter how loose it was around my neck, it still seemed tight and restrictive. Then one day as I was again going to try and wear one, a vision came to me. As the turtleneck sweater went over my head, I saw myself being hung.

It wasn't a scary thing, just a "matter of fact" vision. I then realized I didn't like any high necked cloths because it was bringing back the remembrance of that hanging. I talked to myself and let myself know I wasn't going to get hung in this life time and put the sweater on. There was a totally different feeling this time. I wore the sweater all day and when that old uncomfortable feeling came up, I just reminded myself it was from a past life.

We can also do this with emotions we are trying to understand. Let's say you are a very jealous person in this lifetime. You're so jealous if your friends talk to other people you get angry. If your lover even looks at another person you accuse them of having an affair. You're also jealous of people who have money or nicer things than you do. You're just one jealous person.

Then you die and get to look at your life from the other side. It's then you realize how much time and life energy you've wasted on jealousy. You see how you've hurt people and casued pain and suffering for others through your words or actions. As you watch this life review, you learn you didn't have to be jealous and saw it got you nowhere.

This lesson would be stored in your energy body and not in your brain because your brain is already dead and buried with your body. However because this life and lesson is stored in your energy body, you can bring it forward into your next re-incarnation.

When you come back in a hundred years and because you didn't learn the lesson of jealousy on the human plain, the Universe brings it to you again but you recognize it right away. You feel you don't have to be jealous of others, in fact you think it's a waste of time and energy. Where did you get that feeling or knowing from? It has to be a memory from your energy body.

The lesson is now learned. You just brought it forward to help you in this lifetime. You can now move through it and not have to learn it again. This is why each of us are learning and doing different things all the time. However be aware there are different degrees of lessons too. There are all kinds of jealousy issues or fears and they might be something very small we can work through quickly or they may be something that will take a life time or even two.

One life time we fear spiders and the next lifetime we love them but fear snakes. It takes hundreds of lifetimes to learn all the lessons there are to learn and experience all we can experience.

There are other things we can learn by accessing the memories of our souls. I once had a friend who had a birth mark on his forearm and had always wondered why he had it. He asked me to look into his past lives to see if something came up. Right away I got an image from his energy body. I saw him in a war and he was just outside the walls of a castle. The army he was with was trying to put up ladders so they could scale the wall and get inside. He was at the bottom of the wall holding one of the ladders.

There was confusion and anger. Then he looked up to see boiling oil coming at him from the top of the walls. He raised his left arm in a natural reaction to shield his face. The hot oil hit his arm first and then burned his head and body as it soaked into this cloths. Death was slow and painful.

When he came back into this life time, his soul remembered this painful event and marked it with a birth mark so he would one day remember it and the lesson he learned. He was thrilled with the reading because he had had dreams of this event and wondered why. Now he knew. But what was the lesson?

A major part of this lesson was not to let others lead him blindly into a dangerous situation. In this present life time he is a person who thinks about every move and he is a non-conformist. He had learned the lesson but is now at the other end of the spectrum. Maybe in his next life time he'll learn to be balanced with this lesson.

When we reincarnate, it brings new lessons, experiences and life to us; just like each new day brings new things our way. I don't understand why more people can't see this. We are life in a human form but there are thousands of ways life is expressed. I'm sure in each solar system and galaxy there are all kinds of different life forms. I remember a scene from Star Wars where a human walks into a bar on another planet and he's the only human in the place. The bar is filled with all kinds of strange looking life forms. It's pretty cool really.

While we're in our energy body form we can shape shift, move and create in a totally different way as we travel freely through space. We learn just how powerful we are. We can do it here on Earth too but because there are rules that govern gravity, weight, space and time, it makes it much harder to do.

So in the long run of things, which is millions and billions of years, we hold on to what we are supposed to hold on to in our energy body. Because a memory can be as small as the head of a pin, we have lots of room to store lifetimes of experiences and memories. I even think we have some of our outer space and different planet memories in our energy bodies too.

If our energy body is as tall, wide and thick as our human body, and our memories are stored in a space of energy as small as the head of a pin, look at what we can store. It would take a very long time to full up that much space. One lifetime might fill the space of a big toe. And if we have the ability to compress our energy and then expand it, this could mean we could store even more. It would be like a zip file on a computer.

Our experiences might take up a very small space but we then close them down into a smaller space and when we need them we expand them so more of the energy comes forward. This could explain why we don't remember a lot of things too. We have to unlock or open those files, just like learning about witches might have helped us remember something about a past life.

These small bits of energy can hold powerful memories. It might take a dream to help you remember something stored in your energy body. It might be someone saying something to you or it could be something you think you remember. It could be an experience that opens the file and allows the memory to come flowing out.

It might be a little scary at first but welcome the information. You don't have to do anything with it, just let it be information for you to use when you need it. Just like knowing that 2 + 2 = 4 in this universe. We don't think anything of it and it's as natural as it can be. A past life remembrance can be the same way.

Just because we remember something from a past life doesn't mean we have to act on it. Use the remembrance for this life time so you don't have go through the same lessons over and over again. That is where past life information can be helpful but don't think you're going to remember every detail or even every life. That isn't necessary nor is every detail of a life important, only the lessons.

If we have billions and trillions of years of memories stored up in our energy bodies, then it would take more than one life time to access it and learn from it. We'll remember what we're supposed to remember in a situation or in a life time. Don't worry about it and don't think it won't come to you.

Too many people are focused on wanting to learn about their past lives and not focused on what is happening to them in the present moment. We aren't supposed to focus on the past, whether it's yesterday or 1000 years ago. We're supposed to be living in the present.

If we live in the past or in the future, we miss today. The more we live in the present the more memories we can store in our energy body. We already have the ones from the past stored, so we don't need to dwell on them. We can't store any memories from the future because every time the future comes to us, it's the present. We can only record and store what's happening to us now, at this present moment in time because nothing else really exists.

The past is gone and the future hasn't come yet. This might be the best reason to live in the present moment and try to take it all in. Really live every moment of love, excitement, wonder, good times, uncomfortable times and every lesson we are learning. Take everything in and let your senses experience it. Let every minute count. Let every minute fill your mind, body and soul. Let it be whatever it is, just how it is and experience it. Let it flow into the memory banks of both your human brain and your soul's energy body. Let every moment count.

As I watched my dad lay in the hospital dying, he said, "I've had a good life. Wish I had a couple more years but it's not going to happen. I have no regrets. I'm just going to miss you."

There are many reasons we don't remember every life and every minute of every life but the most important reason is we are living a different life now. We are here today to record different memories and learn different lessons to help us in future life times. Besides, our human brain couldn't take it all in anyway. Maybe someday we'll use all our brain and then we'll be able to remember more.

What if and Maybe

What if we are part of a continuum that works like this –

"Our Universe was formed billions of years ago from its self. Our universe had already been a universe but had burned out and become a black hole, which had laid dormant for about billion years or so. All the life force particles that had been in the universe and on the planets were caught in the implosion when the universe lost its sun. These particles of life had lain dormant for billions of years because the black hole had no light or source of energy.

Then a power source, say a star that was big enough to be considered a sun traveled by the black hole. The energy from the sun sparked some energy in the black hole and things begin to happen. The life force particles took in more and more energy from this sun until it was so full of energy, it exploded and started forming another universe. All the life form particles absorbed energy too. They started forming life in whatever form the DNA told them to be. As the planets cooled and formed and evolved, so did the life forms on the planets."

What?

Here's just one theory scientists are trying to prove. Our universe was a different universe billions of years ago with a different sun. We lived on a planet in this universe until the sun burnt out and it imploded into its self and became either a black hole or a super nova.

It took billions of years for the black hole to regain enough power to explode with a "big bang" and start making a new universe. As this new universe formed, all the microscopic life forms that had survived the last implosion started gathering energy too. Over the next 10 billion years or so, as they gathered more and more energy from the new sun, they formed life on a planet called Earth. Science is proving that this process has been going on for billions of years in galaxies everywhere and we are just now starting to understand it.

What if these specks of life are just that, the spark our soul needs to start the transformation of becoming something else. What if these particles are really the basis of our human, animal and planet kingdoms? What if our soul just floats around from universe to universe until it comes to a place it's wants to visit and explore?

However maybe the rules of space say once you go to a universe, you have to stay there until it dies. That would explain why we keep coming back. We need to stay here until our sun burns out and then we are free to go and try something else. That doesn't mean we can't go anywhere we want too on the other side, it just means we have a 12 billion year contract we have to fulfill in this universe.

If we use this as an example of how universes rebuild themselves, then there really is no death or end to anything. It's all a transformation and then a renewing of what is already there. It might also explain why we all have elements of copper, iron and other minerals in our bodies; many of the same elements that make up Earth. What it doesn't explain or answer is anything about a "God" or the gods, angels, spirits and life after death.

I've had too many things happen to me not to believe in life and life after life. Even my dad as he lay dying looked at the end of his bed and carried on a conversation with his dad, who had been crossed for 50 years. He talked to his deceased mother and saw dogs sitting by other patients' wheelchairs. I have to believe he was seeing the deceased pets of these people who were waiting patiently for their former owners to die and be with them. So I believe in the afterlife but what is that after life?

I've talked to a lot of people on the other side and most are in peace and love it. They show me how they can create anything they want too out of energy. They do what they want and travel where they want. When I ask them about God, they show me a bright light. When I ask them about angels, I can see Light forms and feel an amazing love surrounding me. I know there is more to life than just some space dust and particles and maybe even our souls don't come from outer space but from a different dimension.

That brings up another question – are we even from this dimension? What if we aren't descendants from the Lemurians or from any other life from in this dimension? What if we were created in a different dimension, say the fourth dimension? We go back to a place that can't be seen clearly from this dimension, so maybe we were created in that dimension and we are only visiting this dimension to experience it? It seems that God and angels are in a "different place" than we are so maybe that's were we have to go when we are done here.

Many people believe there are as many as 12 different dimensions or more on the other side of the veil. Maybe we were created in one of them. What if we're all aliens from a different dimension? What if we have to come to different planets in different solar systems to meet in one common dimension? What if each universe has a central meeting planet where we can learn from each other? What really happens when a universe dies?

When universes implode at the end of their lives, maybe they are thrown into another dimension too. Maybe there is so much power in the implosion some of the specks of life that were on the planets in that universe get caught and stored in another dimension. It looks like a black hole to us but maybe it's just resting in that dimension. What if these specks of matter are the solid particles that start life in a physical form? Maybe without them we would stay energy all the time and be caught in our own dimension. What if these specks of matter are the eggs of different forms of life? What if they are where we get our blueprint for being human or animal or plants. These specks of life aren't us but are some kind of life we agree to become.

This would explain how we can be a human yet have a soul that never dies. It would also help us see that God, or what greater power there is, is bigger than we can imagine. It not only rules this universe but all of space and other dimensions. If this is true, then we're part of that power whether we are in human form, spirit form or "alien" form.

If these life form particles are in every universe and different dimensions, then there has to be life on other planets. What if we get to pick a universe, live there until it implodes and then move to another one to do the same thing? And what if while we're in spirit we're picking up more energy and more learning to bring that knowledge to the universe we are going to reincarnate in?

We don't know many things about this universe, after all, humans haven't been on Earth long enough to know that much. We're really very dumb about how the universe works but we are learning and exploring new things everyday. Our history is changing as we learn more about this planet, the universe and our own human history. Each day there are old civilizations uncovered and now discoveries are explaining Earth's past. We are still guessing at many things and there's much more to uncover and learn.

Writing this book has brought me so much knowledge and a new understanding of life and how it works. It's like when I found out about "dark matter." I had said earlier in the book I thought even empty space had something in it. I didn't know about "dark matter" when I had written this. After I was writing about what could be in the empty spaces between planets and our internal organs, I saw a program on the Discovery channel about this very subject.

I was writing about something I really knew nothing about when I heard a message in my head to go look at the TV. There it was, a program on "dark matter" and how science was starting to study it. The program was talking about how scientists are starting to prove there are no real voids anywhere. Many times these voids are filled with something called "dark matter".

This "dark matter" is between and around all of us and in space. These dark particles don't react like light matter and they are trying to prove that even when we don't see something in the air, it's there. This dark matter has a nick name of "wimps" - which stands for "Weakly Interacting Massive Particles".

They call them that because they don't seem to unite with any other particles. They just do their own thing. Theory has to that they move much faster than the speed of light and they can move through anything, even our bodies.

I think this dark matter makes sense because there is "light matter" to counter it. I'm now wondering if duality is everywhere, not just here on Earth or in our Universe but in space and in every universe. Is duality a condition of the laws of space? Where there's light does there have to be dark? Where there's good does there have to be bad? Where there's life does there have to be death? Is this what every universe in space is about?

Science is just on the tip of the iceberg in starting to prove there are no voids. Every space has something in it. We know here on Earth every space is taken up with something, even if it's just air. We have also created airless vacuums in science to see what would happen without the presence of air. These vacuums have been considered "empty" until the discovery of dark matter. Now science is looking at dark matter as something that fills and floats through even these man made voids.

Dark matter seems to be everywhere there isn't light and in some cases even between light. These particles don't fit or form together to make anything solid so we can't see them. And as it is with most humans, if you can't see it, then it must not exist.

Well, science has built some amazing equipment and labs just to try and catch these dark particles. Because they seem to move through everything and react to nothing, they haven't been able to stop them long enough to study them. This just proves we are still in our infancy in learning about matter and space.

Looking out into space is like looking out into the ocean. We know there is something more out there, but we can't see it nor do we really understand how far away it is. There seems to be nothing between us and the next land mass but water and empty space. This is what we think about outer space and the "space" between two planets. We think there's nothing there, just a void of darkness.

However, this is where the "WIMPS' come in. Science is proving there is something in this vast space between planets and even here on Earth between land masses. It will take years, generation and maybe even eons to know or prove what is really floating around out there, but I'm sure one of these days we will have an answer, after all that's part of being here. We can lay out the best plans and come up with theories but we aren't real certain about many things in space or even how big "space" is.

So how much space is out there?

Let's look at what a universe does to get a general idea of the magnitude of space. Science is proving that universes move thru space; they aren't stationary. Science calculates a universe can move thru space at about 3000 miles a minute. If only one universe moves at that speed for only a thousand years that would be approximately 1,576,800,000,000 miles it has traveled.

Now take that number and times it by 20 to 100 billion years, depending on each universes' life, and that's about how far one universe or galaxy moves through space during its life time. Then take that number and apply it to 100,000 other universes or galaxies in every direction. Than remember that each galaxy could be about 16 million light years across or larger so they take up that much space just being a galaxy. That will give you an idea of how big "space" is. I'm not sure we have a number that big.

This is too much for our human brain to understand or even think about. It's also hard for our ego to take in as we want to be the only ones in space and we want to control it. What a laugh that is! We're only one small galaxy moving thru space. Look at it as a peanut in the ocean.

Our galaxy is moving, changing and expanding like every other galaxy out there. As we study other galaxies, we can put some of what we learn back into learning more about ours. Nothing is ever in the same place because our galaxy is never in the same place. It's just in space like the other thousands of galaxies. What's really funny is we think we're the only life forms in this massive expanding area we call space. The probability of this being true is extremely low. Do we really think we are the only life forms in a place so big we can't even see the end or even imagine the end of it? What an ego humans have!

Okay, so if there's something much bigger going on in outer space than we can comprehend, what's the point?

The point is if every galaxy collapses in on its self in some way at some time, then in a million years or so builds its self back into a new galaxy and life starts all over again, even space has no end. The whole point is there is no end. We don't have to fear anything because we are taken care of and live forever no matter what. The point is life is life and we are life in all forms.

There is just no end. Even if we are only made from a speck of dust in a new galaxy, that speck of dust has to have our life form in it to make the form we need to take to experience what we can in that Universe. Everything from that first rebirth is then evolving into whatever it wants or needs to become.

If this is true, our souls truly are an energy form that can float around in space and attach to whatever universe or galaxy we want to be attached too. Why? Because our soul is not made from the same elements as any universe. Only the bodies we choose to ride around in are made from the elements of the universe that exploded. Our soul just picks up the life form particles and we become that life form. Why? I feel we need to be in a body that has some elements of the planet we are on because they body has to survive on that planet and having some of the same elements keeps the vibration of the Earth right so the body can survive here. The particles in our bodies that hold some of the same elements of Earth vibrate at the same rate so the body feels safe on Earth. **These particles are the life form, our soul is the life.**

So if we are the descendants of the first Lemurians, where did they come from? Could the life force particles they used to form life on Earth be the same particles that still brings life to Earth now? Could these particles be from the last time our galaxy burned out then imploded, built up energy and then exploded again? Could part of these particles be the dark matter of space and travel thru time collecting energy to bring them to life? Have we lived in this galaxy before it became a black hole and then renewed its self? Is this the true meaning of resurrection?

If so, where does God fit in? Well in my opinion, God is still the force looking over the massive place we call space. If God is so great he can make our Earth and everything on it, what makes us think he is limited to just this galaxy? Are we that naïve? And what if we are so much part of this greater power that we are "gods" in our own right? What if we're just baby gods trying to learn our power and grow up? What if we really do have as much power as God? Is this why we have so much free will?

Ever think about why we have free will? I think it's because whoever or whatever made us is way too busy to run our lives for us. They are busy creating more for us to enjoy. They know the master plan is live and experience and then travel somewhere else and do the same thing again. They know there is no death so they know we can't fail or even leave them. Even dark entities live in space, which is still part God or the whole and are not really separate from the same force that created us.

So if this theory is correct, we are like the Phoenix; a mythical bird that bursts into flame when it's old and has received all the knowledge of its life time. It burns up and becomes just ash. However, out of the ashes it soon rises to become more powerful and beautiful than it was in its previous life. Are we like this bird? Do our bodies burn up when the universe does but our souls go out into space to seek out other life particles in other universes so we can become a solid form again?

What if there is some truth to all the myths and legends that humans have written about for thousands of years? Since this chapter is called "what if", let your imagination run wild with all the possibilities about the past and "what ifs". Boggles the mind, doesn't it.

What if some of us go to different universes after we die looking for other life force particles to take in and become. What if this is where we mix our energy particles with other energy particles to make different beings. There are some many possibilities and endless theories we can't even being to talk about them here.

If we really believed we were just specks of light matter waiting for enough energy to come along and help us grow, we would be no better than a plant. Plants don't have brains. They do have DNA that tells them what they are and what they're supposed to do but they don't think about it. It's in their cellular blueprint.

Well, we have DNA and a cellular blueprint but we also have something a plant doesn't, a soul. A plant has energy around it because it's made up of moving atoms and cells and all kinds of other microscopic energies, but it doesn't have a soul. I feel the difference between plants and animals is the soul. The soul is what picks up the DNA and cellular blueprint from the life force particles in any universe. Not the other way around.

The soul is pure energy and that makes it more alive than most things we are familiar with. However to bring the soul into a physical life form where it can learn different things, it has to "pick up" a physical life form so to speak. It's like crawling into a shell and growing into whatever was in the shell in the first place. This makes so much sense to me because if we are the descendants of the Lemurians, they were shape shifters and were the first beings here on Earth to take solid form by entering different objects that had already gathered enough energy to become solid.

I think the Lemurians soon learned the soul couldn't really live in a tree. It needed more creative ability and more movement to be happy. Is this why to this day we have to have movement and be creating to be happy? The Lemurians must have looked around at the life force particles that were here on Earth and saw they could become and evolve into a form we now call human. It wasn't perfect and still isn't but we're a very young species and still have billions of years to work on it.

However, becoming human seemed to be the only life form on Earth where a soul could live, learn and create in the way it wanted. I don't have proof on this but it makes sense that if every universe holds its own life force particles then we have to become whatever those particles tell us to become. Maybe souls don't have DNA, they are just energy. Maybe we need these "seeds of life" to become something else, just like the flowers. Maybe we are from different dimensions and we want to experience as much as we can. Maybe we have as much driving force to explore and create as the Power that created us.

Having a soul means you have emotions. You cry, you laugh, and you get angry, happy and all other kinds of things. Animals have souls too. Where do you think they were created? If God made them, then wouldn't they have to be made in the same place we were made? (I'm talking souls here not physical form.)

Everything on Earth has some kind of life to it because of the atoms and other elements it's made of. Everything we see is made of these atoms and things we don't understand. Everything we see is made from "light matter" and this matter has rules it follows. Everything we don't see could be "dark matter" which has its own rules to follow. Dark matter, as we discussed earlier, is what we don't see or understand and yet it can hide many things.

Maybe that's how the cloaking devises worked in Star Trek. The enemy knew how to surround its self with dark energy just like the Universes do. However, this would seemly take some real work and knowledge of the dark matter because, as I stated before, dark matter doesn't seem to act like light matter. It isn't attracted to its self or light matter. Scientists think, but it's not proven, that this dark matter isn't affected by gravity or anything else for that matter, so getting it to act like a cloaking device might be stretching it a bit.

There has to be a reason for dark matter even if it's just to balance light matter. Everything here has some purpose or meaning, everything. So if light is needed, so is dark. Both light and dark matters are elements that create some kind of balance that we will probably discover in another thousand years.

We need light to live. Many of us get depressed if we don't have enough light. Maybe we understand this "dark matter" on a soul level. Maybe because we live with dark matter in outer space when we die, we understand it and really know about it. Maybe we like the light matter better because we can create more with it than with the dark matter. Maybe because the dark matter is individual particles that don't seem to form together we can't create anything from it.

Is this why we are so opposed to "dark" beings, dark rooms and other dark things? Is this why in spirituality we are always trying to bring more light into our bodies? Does more light help us grow and renew ourselves? Is Light the main factor in our evolution?

According to "Victims of Crimes" surveys and other data, approximately two-thirds of all rapes and sexual assaults occur at night. Same for motor vehicle theft.

When it comes to violent crimes like assault and murder, they usually happen just at sunup or sundown. Most property crimes occur during the day because people are at work and the opportunity is right.

So does dark matter have anything to do with our dark side? It will take another million years to figure that one out and if all of space is filled has dark matter, can that theory be true? After all, God lives somewhere out there and he's supposed to be full of light.

As I said in the beginning of the book, much of what I've written about can not be proven or science is just now starting to study it. Maybe in another thousand years we'll understand more about who we are and what we're doing here - then again, maybe not. Maybe we're supposed to have some blind faith just so we can grow and learn. If we knew everything, there would be no point to anything.

I only know the world we live in is a wonderful, amazing place that we take for granted everyday. I know we're here to learn, experience, grow, evolve and question everything that happens to us. We are here to imprint more information into our soul and then move on to something else. I feel that's what our creator(s) are doing and because we are part of that power, we must do the same. It's part of our blueprint.

As God/Goddess creates more worlds and universes, we explore and roam the world of space. It's endless. It's suppose to be an adventure, fun and more than we think it really is. As a soul, we have no limitations. As a human, we have limited ourselves to what others think we are supposed to be like. Then we focus on the "what ifs".

We start thinking "what if I make a wrong or unwise choice?" "What if it doesn't turn out right?" "What if it does turns out right?" "What if someone doesn't like me?" "What if they like me too much?" "What if, what if, what if?" STOP!

We should learn to let it go. We shouldn't worry about the "what ifs" because a "what if" is living in the future. If we project too much of the "what if" energy into the future, that's exactly what we'll get back – what if! You don't want that to happen because the energy around "what if" is an unsettled energy of not knowing. This will make your future unsettled and unknowing.

There's nothing known about "what if" and "maybe". It's all speculation. It's all guessing. Do you really want to bring that kind of energy into your life everyday? Wouldn't you rather bring in a positive, knowing energy?

When you say to yourself, "I know if I want this to work I have to follow it thru to the end. I have to be the one to make the choices and do what I want to do no matter what someone else thinks."

This kind of thinking is what life and learning is all about. This kind of thinking and action will bring you more energy and light to get things done and move thru your life. Everything you do isn't going to turn out the way you want because if it did, you wouldn't learn half the things you are supposed to learn in this life. Life is getting what you want and not getting what you want. It's great.

Let go of the "what ifs" and the "maybes" and watch what happens in your life.

As we come to the end of this book, know it's really just a beginning. Hopefully you'll explore more on your own. I hope your mind will be more open to all the opportunities and adventures we have here on Earth. Whether science can prove or disprove some of the things I've written about, they are my opinions and feelings and there is no wrong or right about them.

Live your life as there is no right or wrong, there "just is" and you'll find a wonderful world. Everything is just like it's supposed to be according to the master plan. All universes are operating in the way they are supposed too. A much more powerful force is making sure of that. All we really need to do is relax, enjoy and learn as much as we can so when we move on, we can take all that knowledge with us to use somewhere else. And whether we're from this universe or another dimension isn't the point or the problem; it just is.

May all your adventures be great

May all your lessons be learned

May all your miracles be appreciated

May all your days be filled with joy and wonderment

May you treat people like you want to be treated

May you live your life like it's your last one

May you understand how powerful you are

May you find whatever it is you are looking for in this life

So how old are we? Only God knows for sure and He's not talking.

About the Author

Shirley Scott lives in Walla Walla, Wa where she does clairvoyant readings from her home in person, on the phone or by email. She has been doing readings for both animals and people for over 11 years and is always studying and learning more about how energy works in our body, mind and in the physical world we live in.

She lives with her 3 dogs and 6 cats and volunteers at the Washington State Penitentiary to train the inmates to train dogs. Part of her Spiritual work it to help dogs who are at the humane society get trained and then adopted into forever homes. She also has her own 501c3 rescue for animals. She is currently looking for 10 acres to build a rescue ranch for animals and to make a space to rehabilitate animals as well as giving workshops on animal welfare, safety, training, communication and other issues.

To find out more about Shirley or her rescue ranch vision, please go to www.animaltalkhealing.com or www.animalrescueranch.com